"A refreshing and definitive look at God's instructions to couples on how to live sacrificially—for each other and for their families."

Dennis Rainey, executive director,
Family Life, Campus Crusade for Christ

"Wielding his biblical scalpel with careful thoroughness, Bryan Chapell cuts to the heart of selfishness, irresponsibility, and abuse that mar so many supposedly Christian marriages today. More than that, he marks out the path of self-denying love in marriage with a firm hand, and provides discussion questions to ensure that couples who have read the book have grasped its message. This exposition can do nothing but good."

J. I. Packer, author, theologian

"*Each for the Other* is one of the few indispensable books on marriage. Because of its biblical precisions and practical sensitivity, it is sweetly radical and bracing. Here is the landscape of marriage as it ought to be. This is a book to read, reread, and savor; a first-class achievement."

R. Kent Hughes, senior pastor, College Church in Wheaton

"A marvelous treatment of the biblical model for and teaching on the family."

R. C. Sproul, author, theologian

"The best book I've read on the biblical view of family. It is refreshing in this day of 'how-to' books to also learn the 'whys' of God's concerns for the family."

Vesta Sproul, author

"Devoid of tiresome clichés and performance-based stereotypes, *Each for the Other* is a refreshing study of what marriage can be when the gospel captures the hearts of a husband and wife, and grace fuels their intimacy. This encouraging book once again convinced me that marriage, like all of life, is to be lived out of the extravagant supply of God's love for us in Christ."

Scotty Smith, senior pastor, Christ Community Church,
Franklin, Tennessee; author, *Objects of His Affection*

"This book is the most thorough exposition of Ephesians 5:22–6:4 that I have read. It covers not only the husband and wife relationship but also that of parent and child. It is thoroughly scriptural, balanced, and fair to husband and wife, parent and child."

Jerry Bridges, author, *The Discipline of Grace*

"There are so many books on marriage, and most of them are nonsense. They are either too lofty to help or too silly to abide. This one is profound, so if you read only one book on marriage, make this one it. Biblical, realistic, and practical. You'll thank me for recommending it to you."

Steve Brown, president, Key Life radio program;
professor, Reformed Theological Seminary

"The insights are profound but simple, and the distinction between submission as power and submission as grace is quite helpful."

Michael Horton, author, theologian, editor of Modern Reformation

"I have used this book in premarital counseling and have seen it shape couples' perspectives on the incredible intricacies of the marriage relationship. I have used it with married couples who are on the verge of trashing their whole relationship and have seen it pinpoint their selfishness and self-centeredness. . . . This is a tool that you will want to have at your disposal, that it may do a work in your life and be used in the lives of others. . . . This is a book I will want to read over and over again."

George Mitchell, chairman, Christian Education Committee,
Presbyterian Church in America (PCA)

"As I read Each for the Other, I had the sense of finding something for which I had long looked. The church is in desperate need of a teaching tool to help God's people build marriages that reflect the reality of his grace. I think this book is that tool. Bryan combines theological precision with tender practicality and passionately presents the need for and God's provision of grace in our marriages. This book is a must-read for every married couple and for every person considering marriage."

Susan Hunt, author; past director of Women in the Church,
Presbyterian Church in America (PCA)

"In a culture that often depreciates or functionalizes the marriage relationship, Bryan Chapell calls Christian couples to live beyond themselves in living out the gospel for one another. By reminding a husband, for example, that 'headship has strings attached,' and by encouraging a wife to honor her spouse 'not because of the goodness he possesses, but because of the grace he needs,' this book invites both partners to commit themselves to becoming conduits of God's sacrificial love for one another and for their children. Each for the Other is balanced, refreshing, practical, and thoroughly biblical."

Nancy Groom, author, Married without Masks
and Heart to Heart about Men

EACH
FOR THE
OTHER

*marriage as it's
meant to be*

REVISED EDITION

BRYAN CHAPELL
WITH KATHY CHAPELL

BakerBooks
Grand Rapids, Michigan

© 1998, 2006 by Bryan Chapell and Kathy Chapell

Published by Baker Books
a division of Baker Publishing Group
P.O. Box 6287, Grand Rapids, MI 49516-6287
www.bakerbooks.com

Printed in the United States of America

Library of Congress Cataloging-in-Publication Data

Chapell, Bryan.
    Each for the other : marriage as it's meant to be / Bryan Chapell with Kathy Chapell.—Rev. ed.
        p.   cm.
    Includes bibliographical references. (p.).
    ISBN 10: 0-8010-6601-8 (pbk.)
    ISBN 978-0-8010-6601-6 (pbk.)
    1. Spouses—Religious life. 2. Marriage—Religious aspects—Christianity.
    I. Chapell, Kathy. II. Title.
    BV4596.M3C48 2006
    248.8′44—dc22   2006005990

Unless otherwise indicated, Scripture quotations are taken from the HOLY BIBLE, NEW INTERNATIONAL VERSION®. NIV®. Copyright © 1973, 1978, 1984 by International Bible Society. Used by permission of Zondervan. All rights reserved.

Scripture marked KJV is taken from the King James Version of the Bible.

Names of individuals and occasional specifics are changed in some personal accounts appearing in this book to respect the concerns and wishes of those involved. My debt is great to those who have taught me the realities of Christ's love by the testimony of their lives.

To Kathy, my wife, whose love yields
joy,
strength,
comfort,
courage,
and
faith.

In loving her, I find more of
myself,
more ability to love,
and
more of the love of my Savior.

Through her love, our children,
Colin,
Jordan,
Corinne,
and
Kaitlin,
bring us joy, pride, humility, and more faith.

In my absences, Kathy has been our family's heart.
In my busyness, she has been our care.
In my awkwardness, she has been our tenderness.
We rise up and call her God's great blessing
on our home (see Prov. 31:28).

Contents

INTRODUCTION

Who's in Charge?

T HEY KNEW THEIR relationship was coming apart when they came to see me. Though each claimed to be trying to "do what the Bible says," love had drained from their marriage. The reason was not obvious. Both had come from church families and both were well schooled in Scripture. They had even met at a Christian college. I detected nothing in their backgrounds that could account for their current tension.

I asked the young man for his own explanation of their troubles. He expressed consternation. He said that he had tried to be a good husband. Because his college had emphasized following biblical family models, he had committed himself to being a spiritual leader in his home. I asked him how he expressed his leadership. This is what he said:

> In order to make sure there is no question about who is the head of our home, I make sure both my wife and I let Scripture

rule our actions. For instance, when I come home from work, I want to relax. Still, I try to act as the head of my home. If my wife asks for some help in the kitchen, or with the kids [he had three preschoolers, including a set of twins], I don't immediately drop my newspaper and snap to attention. To make clear who is the head of our home, I flip a coin in my mind. If it comes up heads, I help. If it comes up tails, I don't. That way there's no question of who's in charge.

Now I thought I was beginning to get an idea of where some of the problems in this marriage might lie. But why? Though this man's attitude may seem extreme, the Bible does say that the husband is the "head" of the home. Scripture gives a husband a right—even a responsibility—to keep spousal roles clear. So how do we know this man's conduct was wrong?

Finding answers to this question will require us to go beyond a surface reading of Scripture. We will see that the Bible never justifies dictatorial rule by one spouse or requires the abandonment of personal dignity by another.

The Glories of Sacrifice

Access to the deeper dimensions of the Bible's instruction requires no special revelations. Hearts open to the message of Scripture will recognize that God neither commends nor commands selfishness. When the prince of heaven gave his life to rescue us from our sin, he taught us the glory of sacrifice. Jesus said, "Whoever finds his life will lose it, and whoever loses his life for my sake will find it" (Matt. 10:39). Lives devoted to serving self cannot avoid making one's own desires the god of every action. Such gods ultimately enslave us to our own appetites and deprive us of the relationships that make our lives fulfilling.

A marriage built on the foundation of persons finding happiness by using one another ignores the deepest passions God has placed in our hearts by his Spirit. We discover the happiness God intends for our lives only when we use the resources and privileges God has given us for the good of another. By exercising the sacrificial love Christ exhibited, we deepen our understanding of God's care, discovering our value even as we affirm others'.

A brown plaster plaque that hangs in our home represents to my wife and me this sacrificial love. The plaque was an inexpensive wedding present. We initially received it with little interest, not realizing that we would later treasure it. In our early married life of many home moves, we hung the plaque on various walls or displayed it on bookshelves. Other wedding presents such as toasters, blenders, and Crock-Pots eventually gave up the ghost, but somehow the little plaque survived our early nomadic wanderings. It became one of the few constants in our life together and came to symbolize home for us. When we hung that plaque on a wall, it was as though we had carved our initials on the house to say, "This is now officially a Chapell home."

What has made us keep that inexpensive wedding gift throughout three decades of marriage is *not* the beauty of its colors or design (it's just a dull brown, round plaque). We have kept it because of its words: "Home: where each lives for the other, and all live for God." The simple phrases remind us that our happiness comes from giving ourselves to each other and to God. Through the years, we have sought to live what the words say and have known great happiness as a result.

The sacrifice of self does not come easily. The cracks on the plaque remind us that life is full of knocks that threaten the unity God intends for us. And the chips that have been repaired are emblems of the reality that by serving one another according to God's Word, we can overcome difficulties and experience enduring joy.

The Questions of Sacrifice

But what does it mean to serve one another in marriage? Is a man to ignore the Bible's command to be the spiritual leader in the home? Should a woman be a doormat to her husband's demands?

These questions are answered not by discounting what God requires of men and women but by seeing how the instruction to each should benefit the other. Biblical leadership requires a man to place his family's interests above his own. He uses his leadership to enable each member of the family to know the care of God. A woman who submits to such headship is not feeding a man's selfishness but rather is supporting the godly nurture of her family. Neither spouse abdicates biblical responsibilities but rather fulfills the biblical definition of love that "is not self-seeking" (1 Cor. 13:5).

Widespread misunderstanding of these biblical standards, even among those who are trying to do what God requires, is both a cause and a consequence of the family breakdown in our society and the tenacious orientation to self that resides in every heart. Both factors tempt us to dispense with biblical instruction when it does not conform to cultural trends, or to use the Bible selectively to serve our own interests. Not only does this departure from Scripture distance us from the relationships God intends, it also endangers the next generation of families.

Without long-term, Christian models, it is extremely difficult to know at a heart level what God expects in our homes. Neither teaching individuals more Bible facts nor introducing them to the doctrinal distinctives of a particular church will secure the kinds of families God wants. A young man raised in a legalistic home does not automatically know how to be a father and husband because he learns the Greek word for each. A woman neglected by her parents throughout her childhood will still yearn to know if she is nurturing her children correctly long after a three-hour seminar on biblical mothering.

The Standards of Sacrifice

As our secular society continues to assail families, it is critical that Christian homes provide an effective witness for the gospel, ensuring the spiritual well-being of the next generation. Without homes where the sacrificial care of Jesus is demonstrated, the realities of Christian faith will become mere abstractions to our families and thus fail to take root in society.

Statistics published by the U.S. Government well demonstrate the fading reality of selflessness in our homes. In a little more than three decades, the marriage rate (defined as the number of married adults per thousand) has declined by a third; the divorce rate has more than tripled; the percentage of children living with single parents has more than doubled, with a third of children now living without their biological fathers; the number of unmarried-couple households has increased sevenfold; and the percentage of births to unwed mothers has quintupled—accounting now for 35 percent of all births—the highest in the six decades since the government began keeping such figures.[1] While there can be legitimate explanations for individual choices in some categories, taken together, these statistics signal a society where prioritizing self-interest dominates.

The message of Christ's selfless care will not echo in our families unless we adopt values that are radically counter to the me-orientation of the present or the me-Tarzan-you-door-mat stereotypes of the past. This book will help those who are genuinely committed to discovering God's plan for home relationships. In the following pages we will walk through key passages in Scripture where the first Christians were told how to organize relationships. This walk may surprise many. For although the apostolic writers addressed a culture much like our own, they did not call Christians to retreat from society. Instead, the apostles called each Christian to retreat from self.

By teaching us to sacrifice our priorities for the needs of a loved one, the apostles beaconed the truths of Christ's love in ways the world could not ignore. As we live for each other, we reenact the story of Jesus' sacrifice and represent him to one another. That story lifts us from the bottomless pit of self-indulgence to a purposeful life with God.

An example of such sacrificial love surfaced a few years ago in my hometown when two brothers decided to play on sandbanks by the river's edge. Because our town depends on the river for commerce, dredges regularly clear its channels of sand and deposit it in great mounds beside the river. Few things are more fun for children than playing on these mountainous sandpiles—and few things are more dangerous.

While the sand is still wet from the river's bottom, the dredges dump it on the shore. The piles of sand dry with rigid crusts that often conceal cavernous internal voids, formed by the escaping water. If a child climbs on a mound of sand that has such a hidden void, the external surface easily collapses. Sand from higher on the mound then rushes into the void, trapping the child in a sinkhole of loose sand. This is exactly what happened to the two brothers as they raced up one of the larger mounds.

When the boys did not return home at dinnertime, family and neighbors organized a search. They found the younger brother. Only his head and shoulders protruded from the mound. He was unconscious from the pressure of sand on his body. The searchers began digging frantically. When they had cleared the sand to his waist, he roused to consciousness.

"Where is your brother?" the rescuers shouted.

"I'm standing on his shoulders," replied the child.

With the sacrifice of his own life, the older brother had lifted the younger to safety. With similar selflessness the One who is not ashamed to call himself our brother saved us despite our waywardness (see Heb. 2:11). We live eternally by standing before God on the righteousness that Jesus Christ provided at the cost of his own life. This is the grace that God extends to us and that we express to others as we use our resources and privileges for the good of one another.

In the Christian home each person has the mission of sharing the knowledge and experience of God's care. Strength and brains are never abandoned or used for the promotion of self; rather, we apply each for the other.

The Mission of Sacrifice

Such love will not only thrive in our homes, if we submit ourselves to God's Word; such love can also change our world. Living as a Christian family in the midst of a godless society has transforming power. Church historians say that Christianity swept the ancient Roman world not so much because of the arguments of theologians but because of the infectious love evident in Christian families. This spiritual contagion can spread again. As Christ's love changes our families, it also appeals to outsiders who are desperate for answers to their own family problems. As we model God's grace—his unconditional care for the undeserving—others understand more of Christ's love; and we, by representing the Savior, consequently understand and experience more of his love too.

The purpose of this book is to help men and women know how to express God's grace to one another. My goal is not to provide a fix-it recipe for every family problem. Given the complexities of our relationships, I have little confidence in cookie-cutter formulas for happiness. Rather, I intend to focus on the scriptural principles undergirding the relationships of the Christian family. My prayer is that family members will examine these principles and will then apply them to the different decisions, routines, and responsibilities of each unique home.

Though I am a husband and a father of four, I do not write as an expert who has a ready answer for every situation. My mistakes are more than I can number. Christian family models in my background have often been confusing, and my own heart (true to its human nature) resists sacrifice. The thoughts collected here result from my own struggles to understand

God's Word. As I write, I too am listening for the counsel of Scripture because I recognize that the beauty of my marriage and joy in my family depend on our daily application of God's Word.

Because I treasure my wife's understanding of Scripture and have grown in my knowledge of God's love through her, I have asked her to provide her thoughts at key points in this revised edition. I consider Kathy's contribution to be the best addition to this new version. She is a godly woman whose wisdom and heart have nurtured our family well, and her counsel can enrich many other families. She is also funnier than I and not afraid to share her struggles as well as her advice. So where I get too heavy or obscure, readers can count on Kathy to lighten things up and "get real."

A key Bible passage on which much of this book is based appears below. Although many of the phrases are familiar, they do not always receive a sympathetic hearing in our times. I quote them here as an invitation to each reader to check the words of this book against Scripture. Whether your family has spanned decades or is just beginning, you can know the fullness of God's love only as you live in obedience to his Word. Thus any human counsel about family responsibilities should be heeded only to the extent that it conforms to the Bible's teachings. This is what God says:

> Submit to one another out of reverence for Christ.
> Wives, submit to your husbands as to the Lord. For the husband is the head of the wife as Christ is the head of the church, his body, of which he is the Savior. Now as the church submits to Christ, so also wives should submit to their husbands in everything.

Husbands, love your wives, just as Christ loved the church and gave himself up for her to make her holy, cleansing her by the washing with water through the word, and to present her to himself as a radiant church, without stain or wrinkle or any other blemish, but holy and blameless. In this same way, husbands ought to love their wives as their own bodies. He who loves his wife loves himself. After all, no one ever hated his own body, but he feeds and cares for it, just as Christ does the church—for we are members of his body. "For this reason a man will leave his father and mother and be united to his wife, and the two will become one flesh." This is a profound mystery—but I am talking about Christ and the church. However, each one of you also must love his wife as he loves himself, and the wife must respect her husband.

Children, obey your parents in the Lord, for this is right. "Honor your father and mother"—which is the first commandment with a promise—"that it may go well with you and that you may enjoy long life on the earth." Fathers, do not exasperate your children; instead, bring them up in the training and instruction of the Lord.

Ephesians 5:21–6:4

PART I

THE
SACRIFICIAL
HUSBAND

To Scale the Heights

Husbands, love your wives, just as Christ loved the church
and gave himself up for her.

Ephesians 5:25

THE DAY WAS bone-chilling but clear. My brother, Gordon, picked me up at my apartment just as the sun was
coming up, and we headed for the tall rocks and clear rivers
of the Ozark Mountains. Home for a leave from the Air Force,
Gordon had promised to take me mountain climbing.

Specially trained to rescue pilots from any terrain in the world, Gordon told me not to worry that I had no idea how to scale tall cliffs that soon loomed before us. "Just do what I tell you," he said. Ropes and safety harnesses, spikes and hammers, rope clamps and helmets soon emerged from his duffel, and up we went.

We started on the smaller rocks with gentle slopes. There Gordon showed me how to use the rope clamps and spikes. He taught me how to ask for more slack or tension on the rope to make my climb, and how to give the same to my partner to enable him to climb with me. I soon learned that the progress either of us made was integrally related to the actions and responses of the other.

By midday I was feeling confident about our routines, and my brother pointed to the sheer face of a cliff across the valley. "Now you're ready," he said. I gulped but agreed.

We hiked to the cliff, roped ourselves together, and side by side started up. Gordon set the course, but I soon discovered that this did not always mean he was above me. The nature of the obstacles and crevices before us meant that sometimes he advanced ahead of me, and sometimes I preceded him. We gave each other tension or slack depending on what was needed to leverage our bodies up the rock. There was no question of who was in charge, but neither was there any question that the one who led the way sometimes had to let his partner advance ahead of him for both to make progress.

The goal was not for one to stay ahead of the other but for both to reach the top. To do this, the one in charge had to assess his own strengths and limitations (and those of his partner) and adjust accordingly. Had he always insisted on being in front, then neither of us would have made the summit.

How these dynamics play out in a marriage as well as on a mountain is the subject of the following chapters. The partners in a biblical marriage are not usually scaling a mountain, but they must constantly surmount challenges to their union. The challenges of careers and children, finances and failures, relatives and regrets make it unlikely that the same person can be out in front all the time if the marriage is to succeed. Thus we need to assess what responsibility marriage partners bear to help each other reach the summit of godliness and joy God intends. The key thought of part 1 is that a husband cannot fulfill his biblical responsibilities without leading his family by reflecting his Savior and respecting his spouse.

I

A MAN'S RESPONSIBILITY

Servant Leadership

S HE STEALS FROM her family. From the outside they
appear to have an ideal home. The house is beautiful,
the couple is attractive, and the kids are sweet. Inside things
are far from ideal—the wife has a gambling addiction. She
has been to counselors, clinics, and pastors. Nothing helps.
Periodically she breaks into her own family's bank accounts
(or pawns family valuables) and gambles away the money.

Her actions have put her family on the edge of bankruptcy
time and time again. The debts cannot be covered even by her
husband's executive salary. The financial damage done to the
family will take half a lifetime to repair. But the worst damage
is not financial, it is relational. It is impossible to measure the
pain of your own spouse stealing from you, destroying your
family's security, and lying about it for months on end.

What should the husband in this marriage do? Consider first what our society tells him to do. It screams, "Get out of that marriage. You don't have to take this. You don't have to put up with her. Leave!"

This husband has not left. Every time his wife has stolen from him and damaged his future, he has forgiven her and taken her back. Even when she was ready to kill herself—ready to give up on her own life—he has loved her. Like the biblical prophet Hosea who took back his unfaithful wife, my friend has continued to love his wife, despite her failures.

Once I asked this young man why he had not ended this nightmare marriage. His words were simple: "My children need her. But more than that, they need to know their Lord. How can they know of a Father in heaven who forgives them if their father on earth will not forgive their own mother? How can my wife know the love of God if the spiritual leader in this home will not love her despite her faults?"

In Christ's name and for the spiritual good of his family, the man holds on to his marriage. There is nothing more important to him than that his children and wife are spared a hell greater than his own present pain. His priority is that his family would know eternal grace. Thus the husband takes precautions to keep funds from his wife that will feed her weakness. He insists on counseling. He entrusts her with responsibilities that will boost her self-image. He ensures the regular church attendance of his family. He treats his wife with respect, and he loves her.

He uses every aspect of his biblical knowledge and authority to help his wife. In these ways he fulfills his biblical responsibility to be the head of his home even as he sacrifices himself for the good of others.

The Head of the Home

Though the situation described may seem atypical, the husband's conduct exemplifies the responsibility of men in Christian marriage. The husband looks past his own rights to consider what is right for his spouse. He refuses to surrender his leadership role in the family but uses his biblical authority to make sure the family's resources and activities serve the best interests of his wife and children.

The apostle Paul articulates this responsibility to which God calls Christian husbands through a *tension* evident in his classic passage on family relationships. Paul first urges all Christians to "submit to one another" (Eph. 5:21). Then, immediately following this general command for submission to one another, the apostle tells wives to "submit to [their] husbands" because "the husband is the head of the wife" (vv. 22–23).[1]

At first glance the call for mutual submission followed by the announcement that the man is the head of the wife seems to echo George Orwell's infamous line in *Animal Farm* that "all animals are equal but some animals are more equal than others." How can we be in submission to one another when someone is *head* over the other?

There are those who try to dismiss these concerns by claiming that the concept of headship is either (1) subject to Paul's chauvinism or (2) specific to his culture.

Was Paul a Chauvinist?

We cannot accept the first claim—which asserts Paul erred due to his male prejudices—without undermining the authority of Scripture (see 2 Tim. 3:16; 2 Peter 1:20–21). The apostles

Kathy's thought: Okay, here I am, married nearly thirty years to a great guy. Bryan is easy to respect, trust, and live with. Yet we are both independent individuals. I like to think that I am relatively intelligent and capable. I made my own decisions before we were married. So what makes Bryan better qualified than I to head our family? Other than what Scripture says, what makes him "the boss"? This really can be a "sticks in my craw" deal. I'm not just being sassy here; I remember wrestling with these questions during our first years of marriage. Bryan *is* very thoughtful and wise, and I don't recall his ever saying anything like, "Kathy, I *am* the head of the household, you know—so submit!" But there were many times when our views and opinions differed, and I wondered, "Does the Bible really say my husband's way is always right? If we differ on something, should I always give in or be silent? Is that what the Bible (or Bryan) really wants?"

I grew up during the emergence of the women's movement in our culture. Although I come from a traditional background and would not claim to buy into all the attitudes of modern feminism, I know that I have been influenced, positively and negatively. I went to college believing that a woman should have an education and career options, regardless of her marital status. I happily chose not to work outside our home after the birth

continues . . .

claimed that God inspired their writing (see 1 Thess. 2:13; 2 Peter 3:15–16). If they were deluded or deceitful, we would have no confidence in anything they wrote. Such reasoning would make us the judges of the Bible. Thus our preferences would determine what the Bible says, and we would assume the role of God. Knowing my own sin and limited understanding, this is not a role I want to assume.

Rather than picking and choosing what passages of the Bible I want to heed, I am content to listen to the Bible's counsel not to add or subtract from its instruction (see Deut. 4:2; Gal. 1:8; Rev. 22:18–19). I will acknowledge that I may misunderstand what the Bible says, but I will trust that God has not made mistakes in his Word. In this way I can continue to seek and rely on wisdom greater than my own.

Was Paul's Culture Alone Addressed?

The second claim, that Paul's standards for the relationship of men and women applied only to his specific cultural situation, needs serious consideration. There surely are times that the apostle gives instructions limited to his ancient culture. When Paul encourages all Christians to greet one another with a holy kiss (see 1 Thess. 5:26) and when he instructs women to wear head coverings in worship (see 1 Cor. 11:6), he does *seem* only to be referring to cultural practices of his day. I stress the word *seem* because Christians may seriously differ over the degree to which they feel these practices still apply.

> of our children, both for their sake and for my own delight in being with them as their primary nurturer. Still, "submitting"? Ouch. Couldn't we just think of it as two equals, walking side by side, never disagreeing or needing to make decisions or resolve differences? I want to do what God wants, but I don't want simply to bow to some male power play. I need to know what Scripture really says about this headship thing and why it is important.

It can be very difficult to decide how to apply ancient practices, such as the Old Testament instruction to leave the edges of one's fields unharvested so that strangers and the poor in the land can find food (see Lev. 19:9–10). It is not nearly so difficult, however, to discern the abiding principles behind the practices. The edges of fields were to be left unharvested so that God's people would show compassion for the needy. A holy kiss was to be exchanged among all in the church so that favoritism would be shunned and fellowship would be enhanced.

Head coverings also communicated abiding principles but not in signals that we understand today. A woman in the ancient world wore a head covering to signify that she was under the authority of another. By contrast a man did not cover his head to show that he was under the authority of God (see 1 Cor. 11:3–4).[2] These cultural cues were used to communicate biblical principles of authority in the New Testament churches, but the cues no longer communicate the same thing, making their continued practice meaningless.[3] The loss of meaning of the practices, however, does not mean the principles of authority are not still in effect. In the same passage where Paul speaks of head covering, he says, "The head of every man is Christ, and the head of the woman is man, and the head of Christ is God" (v. 3). The fact that what we wear on our head (and why) has changed over time does not mean that a man is no longer under the authority of Christ, nor that Christ is no longer under the authority of God—nor that a woman's relationship to her husband has changed.

More will be said in part 2 of this book about ways the apostles emphasize the perpetual nature of their principles for the way men and women should relate. For the moment, we need only to recognize that where Paul details the responsibilities of men in families, the apostle bases his principles on the nature of the church in relationship to Christ.

Paul says that "the husband *is* the head of the wife as Christ *is* the head of the church" (Eph. 5:23, italics mine). This comparison makes it apparent that if the husband *is* no longer head of the wife, then Christ has no continuing authority over his church.[4] Cavalier dismissal of the principles of authority the New Testament establishes for men and women results in denying Christ's authority.

The apostles intended their instructions for Christian families to have continuing authority for us. This means that the headship principle is valid for today.

What Headship Isn't

Being the "head" of a home does *not* mean *nothing*. By saying that Christ is *head* of the church (see Eph. 5:23), the apostle Paul underscores the importance of headship. Christ's identification as our "head" gives significance and clarity to the word.

Ignoring Responsibility

The Bible says that as the head of his bride, the church, Christ serves as her Savior (see Eph. 5:23). Jesus gave himself to make the church holy, radiant, and blameless (see 5:25–27). Thus headship involves taking responsibility—even to the point of personal sacrifice—for the well-being of another. Such a definition for the head of a family grants nobility to the phrase "being a man." It also renders boyish and immature those images of manliness that idealize personal independence, family disinterest, and a "sportin' life." The Marlboro man and Michelob weekends represent true manhood about as well as a five-year-old in a cowboy hat resembles John Wayne.

The strength of character required to head a home for a lifetime makes masculinity defined only as taking care of self seem childish. As a child I witnessed true manhood in my father, whose job required much time on the road. His travel allowance could have provided rooms and meals that would have made my father's trips quite pleasant. But rather than take advantage of the perks, my father would drive late into the night to get home and be at breakfast with his family. Even then his sacrifice was not finished.

For many years the money saved from my father's expenses was placed into an account to provide for my younger brother, whose learning disabilities limit his independence. My father took seriously his responsibility as head of the home, and he sacrificed to fulfill it.

Excusing Passivity

The biblical head of a family lives selflessly. This description repudiates modern perspectives that make headship a nasty synonym for self-seeking power. Because of Christ's agonizing efforts for us, we know that using headship as an excuse for passivity is wrong. The husband who will not lift a finger to serve his spouse may claim he is exercising the prerogatives of headship, but in reality he is abandoning his biblical responsibility.

A mother of three recently told my wife, "My husband hasn't made a decision regarding our family in two years. He makes no attempt to discipline the children—that's left to me. He never consults me about taking out-of-town work assignments. He comes and goes seemingly without any regard for my feelings or our children's needs. They don't even know him. All he does is come home from time to time and break our routine before leaving again. I don't have three children—I have four."

This wife complains frequently to her husband about his habits. He tells her that in a few weeks he will work out a time they can talk. But he never does. He uses his headship as an excuse for passivity. His headship really means nothing but taking care of himself.

Media and feminist objectors to biblical statements about headship frequently accuse the apostles of endorsing male dictatorships. However, in my experience wives are as frequently distressed

Kathy's thought: This man acted as though his home would go in a deep freeze while he was away. He seemed to believe that somehow his wife and children were just *there*, existing, living in a kind of static situation. He needed to understand that a family is a growing organism. Children's bodies, minds, and emotions develop and grow each day. A wife continues to evolve in her sense of self and her ways of thinking and decision making. The relationships between the children and their mother are building and changing. Yet when this man returned home, he expected to step into a home scene frozen in time as though nothing had changed. What he didn't realize is that while he was gone—either in physical distance or emotional passivity—his family had naturally moved ahead, and without him! His wife once told me that she felt she was steering a huge car of a family, but no one was telling her what the travel plans were. The head of the household needs to be guiding decisions by participating in home life and knowing where his family is at each stage of their journey. He cannot choose merely to exist in the family and lead it.

by their husbands' disinterest. Especially in troubled marriages, men often have a passive disregard for their families. In such homes the woman (typically the more verbal one) may constantly complain to the husband about what he is *not* doing. To keep himself from being disturbed, the man reacts to the verbal pressure by erecting a shell of nonresponsiveness or by immersing himself in interests that insulate him from home concerns. The man may even convince himself that because the Bible makes him the head of his home he has the right to be involved as little as he pleases.

A man may also try to rationalize his passivity with the excuse that he is just being kind. He may tell himself that he is being nice by refusing to confront his wife lovingly about her critical spirit, patterns of anger, or disregard for her responsibilities. But if, in fact, he fails to act because he lacks either the courage or energy to risk disturbing the equilibrium his passivity maintains, then he ignores the responsibilities of headship at the expense of his spouse's and marriage's spiritual health. The choice to disregard spiritual need can be just as destructive as passive disregard. The Bible does not permit men to be uninvolved, disinterested, intentionally deaf, of selfishly blind. Headship requires husbands actively (and graciously) to work for the physical and spiritual well-being of each person in the family.

A husband's passivity can lead to cycles of abuse. A common pattern in abusive marriages is long periods of male passivity interspersed with brief episodes of rage. During the periods of relative calm, the man may respond minimally to his wife's complaints. As a result, the wife may be encouraged to needle her husband more to get further cooperation, but his responsiveness often comes at a high price. Even when he complies with the wishes of his wife, the words that shame him into action may steam inside him. Like an emotional pressure cooker that appears unperturbed from the outside, he is preparing to explode. The placid exterior of the husband camouflages his mounting sense of grievance against the disruption of his personal peace.

When the explosion occurs, the man briefly asserts himself with intense aggression. He may later view the abuse as not typical of himself and, therefore, will feel guilty and apologetic. However, this sense of shame will be further reason for the husband to distance himself from home concerns. Thus he returns to the nonresponsiveness that elicits more verbal needling from his wife and sets up the abuse cycle to repeat.

Men who have made idols of the cultural icons of swaggering independence and managerial machismo have no biblical support. They program their actions and emotions to be self-absorbed, self-contained, and nonresponsive. They define their family role by what they have a right *not* to do. Being a biblical head of a home demands more. Passive avoidance of whatever is bothersome, disquieting, or irksome will not suffice. Indifference to the needs of one's family is not biblical headship. Contrary to some teaching prevalent in both Christian and secular settings, God requires the *active* sacrifice of the head of a home. Biblical headship does not mean nothing.

Wrong Definitions

We cannot ignore Scripture and define headship any way we please.

SOURCE

In our English usage, *head* sometimes means "source," as when we refer to the headwaters of a river. Were we to use this definition, we might decide that "the husband is the head of the wife" (Eph. 5:23) means only that the man — in the person of Adam — preceded his wife in creation (see Gen. 2:21–23).

By this logic, some have argued that the Bible does not say that a husband has leadership responsibilities.[5] Passages dealing with headship are interpreted as referring to our history, not our conduct. Such interpretations enable us to avoid authority issues and fit well with trends that minimize the differences between men and women.

The problem is that *head* does *not* merely mean "source" in the Bible.[6] In the 2,336 instances of the use of this term in ancient Greek literature, there are no clear instances where the word only carries the idea of "source" or "origin."[7] Further, the passages describing the head of the home make it clear that the term involves authority.[8] After all, wives are told to submit to their husbands because man is the head of the wife, even as the church is to submit to Christ because he is her head (see Eph. 1:10, 22; 5:22–24; 1 Cor. 11:3, 10). Even if *head* were only to mean "source" in the Bible,[9] we know that it hardly offends modern sensibilities less for the Bible to say that man is the source of woman.[10]

SUPERIORITY

Just as wrong as underrepresenting the authority of biblical headship is overstating it. Some husbands use their headship as justification for making slaves of their wives. A horror of my pastoral experience was a man who believed the Bible supported his right to torture his wife if she did not submit to his sexual desires. Another man made his wife log her hours of housework to make sure she did not loaf. Of such men Kent Hughes appropriately writes:

> God's Word in the hands of a religious fool can do immense harm. I have seen "couch potatoes" who order their wives and children around like the grand sultan of Morocco—adulterous misogynists with the domestic ethics of "Jabba the Hut" who cow their wives around with Bible verses about submission—insecure men whose wives do not dare go to the grocery without permission, who even tell their wives how to dress. But the fact that evil, disordered men have perverted God's Word is no reason to throw it out.[11]

The Bible requires men to treat their wives with consideration and respect (see 1 Peter 3:7). Headship never grants husbands the right to inflict arbitrary, prideful, or capricious rule on their spouses. The apostle says, "Husbands, love your wives" (Eph. 5:25). He also defines such love: "Love is patient, love is kind. It does not envy, it does not boast, it is not proud. It is not rude, it is not self-seeking, it is not easily angered, it keeps no record of wrongs" (1 Cor. 13:4–5).

Nowhere does Scripture define love as taking advantage of others. The command for husbands to love their wives should rule out any definition of headship that encourages using or harming others. Paul writes that husbands should love their wives "just as Christ loved the church and gave himself up for her" (Eph. 5:25). Jesus' sacrificial ministry—the washing of feet, the giving up of heavenly glory, the suffering on a cross—demonstrates that biblical headship never permits using one's position for selfish benefit.

What Headship Is

Defining headship by saying what it isn't does not answer all our questions. What does the Bible mean when it says that the husband is the head of the wife?

Possessing Authority to Lead

The head of a home *possesses the most authority* in the family. This conclusion is difficult to sidestep when we simply read the Bible without modern prejudices. Paul instructs wives: "submit to your husbands" (Eph. 5:22). Then he gives the *reason* for this submission: "the husband is the head of the wife" (v. 23). Next he offers an *example* of submission: "the husband is the head of the wife as Christ is the head of the church," and "as the church submits to Christ, so also wives should submit to their husbands" (vv. 23–24). Finally Paul indicates the *extent* of the husband's authority: "wives should submit to their husbands in everything" (v. 24).

Clearly the apostle wants the husband to have primary authority (see 1 Cor. 11:3–10; Titus 2:5). The husband's authority, however, does not grant him a right to selfish control. Headship has strings attached. The apostle says that just as the church submits to Christ, so also wives should submit to their husbands (see Eph. 5:22–23). This comparison limits the authority of a husband as well as legitimizing it.

The right to exercise family authority exists only to the extent it reflects Christ's nature and purposes. This does not mean that a wife must only honor the authority of a husband who is a Christian (see 1 Peter 3:1). God bases his marriage instructions on the way he created us, and his standards do not disappear because our marriages are faulty. Rather, right

Kathy's thought: It's very reassuring to me to know that Scripture does not require me to submit to my husband in ways that cause me to disobey or dishonor the Lord. As much as I love my husband, I love—and must love—God first and foremost. If I try to make everything I do a proclamation of my Savior's work in my heart—if I seek to do everything as if serving Jesus directly—then submitting to my spouse is a subset of that work, never a separate work in itself. Whether I am doing the laundry, paying the monthly bills, nurturing the children, pursuing a career, discussing our family's plans for the future—if I know that serving and honoring Jesus is foremost in both of our hearts and minds, then I can submit to my husband as the head of our home, under the headship of the Lord we both love.

ordering of our relationships is one way God brings his beauty into scarred lives. Headship—even flawed headship—is designed to fulfill God's purposes and should be honored. However, when a husband uses his position to counter the purposes of God, then the man has no biblical authority for his actions. The husband who demands that his wife stay in a corner while he abuses their children betrays his biblical authority. Headship that transgresses God's purposes loses God's approval.

A wife has no obligation to submit to her husband when he demands that she disobey God. When Paul tells wives to submit to their husbands as to the Lord in everything, the apostle is not teaching that husbands are divine. The command to submit "as to the Lord" (Eph. 5:22) reminds women that they are ultimately accountable to God. The Bible similarly urges us to work as though we are serving the Lord (see Eph. 6:5; Col. 3:23). In so honoring employers, we do not pretend they are gods, nor should we obey them if they order us to break God's law. In the same way a wife who submits to her husband's authority honors God, but not if by obeying the man she disobeys God. The wife should submit to her husband "in everything" that God's Word approves.

Husband and wife bear mutual responsibility to obey God. Neither can say that he or she has a right to disregard God's standards because of what the other has commanded or neglected. Great harm results when anyone forgets these basic principles. Far into his adult years, a friend I will call Joshua has borne the scars of parents who neglected these principles. Joshua's father worked the late shift as a New York taxi driver. Though he rarely woke from his daytime sleep, the father would occasionally assert his "spiritual authority" when he came home drunk. In those predawn hours the father would awaken his wife and children with beatings in order to "preach the Bible" to them in the living room. To this day Joshua reports that his mother defends his father's actions because "he is the head of the home, and the Bible says we must submit to his wishes."

I have no ready answer for what this long-suffering wife should have done. What I see in her son, however, is a lifetime of turmoil resulting from the perverted definition of headship that a husband portrayed and a wife defended. Having been taught that headship included the right to abuse, Joshua became an abuser of his own wife and children. The cowering of his children finally awakened him to what Scripture really teaches. The Bible never sanctions the actions of a bully in the name of headship. God never approves abuse nor requires submission to it.

Headship receives biblical support only when governed by godly purposes and practices.[12] The responsibilities God places on husbands yields a definition of headship far from the dictatorial rule or disengaged privilege some men want the Bible to justify. *Biblical headship is the conscientious and loving use of the authority God grants a husband to ensure that all in his home honor God and experience his blessings.*

Using Authority to Serve

Biblical headship bears responsibility for others. The head of a home *must use his authority to serve* the good of his family. In this sense, biblical headship requires service. The husband's authority must advance purposes greater than self-interest. Paul makes this clear in the way he writes his instructions. These standards for husbands and wives follow one long sentence in the Greek text. That sentence includes instructions for all persons in the church (see Eph. 5:18–21). Paul first urges everyone to be "filled with the Spirit" (v. 18). Then he explains being filled with the Spirit. Everyone should (1) "speak to one another with psalms, hymns and spiritual songs"; (2) "sing and make music in your heart"; (3) "always giving thanks to God"; and (4) "submit to one another out of reverence for Christ" (vv. 19–21). Everyone who is filled with the Spirit serves others sacrificially.[13]

To flesh out the nature of our service, Paul speaks to three groups: wives and husbands, children and parents, slaves (better translated "servants"; see note 3 in chapter 5) and masters. In each grouping, the first individuals the apostle mentions (i.e., wives, children, and servants) are those his culture would already expect to submit. This is like telling soldiers to obey their officers. The apostle says nothing unsettling for his culture when he tells these individuals to submit.

The radical nature of Paul's instruction appears in what he says to those who are not in traditionally submissive roles. First, Paul affirms their authority. For example, the apostle still gives parents authority over children (see Eph. 6:1–4), and servants are not encouraged to take a vote to decide whether to obey their masters (see vv. 5–8). Yet despite his refusal to annul traditional authority, the apostle will *not* affirm the status quo. He requires people with authority (as well as those in submissive roles) to live sacrificially for those God places in their spiritual care (see 5:1–2, 21, 25).[14]

Paul does not deny the need for obedience from those in traditionally submissive positions, nor does he invalidate the authority of others. Instead, he tells *all* parties to surrender their personal interests to the good of others (see 5:2). The apostle's words are particularly weighty for those who have authority because they have the most adjusting to do in the new social order the Bible establishes. Parents must exercise their authority to serve the good of their children. Masters must care for those who work for them. Heads of homes must consider spouse and family before self.

Paul does not remove authority from the heads of homes, he redefines it. Their authority is not the right to order others around for personal benefit; it is the responsibility to arrange for a family's well-being. Biblical headship uses authority to ensure the good of others. In this sense, the head of a home sacrifices himself for the good of his family. He surrenders his interests to the needs of others.

The Bible cuts across cultural norms that would keep one group of persons pawns of another. Instead, God calls husbands to fulfill the responsibilities of a servant/leader—one whose authority is directed toward providing for the good of others.[15]

Those who perceive headship as synonymous with dictatorship will have trouble understanding this servant/leader calling. Clarity comes, however, when we remember that Jesus came as our servant/leader. He surrendered himself to our needs though he has absolute authority (see Matt. 28:18). Because he who has all authority in heaven and earth came to serve rather than to be served (see 20:28), we know that sacrifice does not erase authority. Instead, when authority serves the interests of another, it masters the purpose for which God ordained it.

Because a husband's headship should reflect the ministry of Christ, the head of a home is Christ's chief representative there. A wife and children should better know the love of their Savior through the head of the home. He is to display Christ's grace, making sure that God's standards guide the family and that his love governs its relationships. In short, the head of a home is to be Christ to his wife and family—Jesus should shine through him. This is an immense responsibility, so overwhelming that it requires every man humbly to seek God's aid.

Only by a close relationship with the Savior and by regular exposure to the mind of God in Scripture will a man know what it means to be the head of a home. A husband should submit his own life to God before he requires submission from anyone else. The true head of a home bows before God, asking to be the man God desires, interceding for the welfare of the family, and petitioning for love, wisdom, and strength that will make God's grace evident in the home. Only when a man humbles himself in these ways can he give a proper account of his headship to God.

In his "Wedding Sermon from a Prison Cell," Dietrich Bonhoeffer, the German theologian who lost his life opposing Hitler, wrote of such headship. Written in 1943, the words ring true today because they resonate with timeless Scripture:

Now when the husband is called "the head of the wife," and it goes on to say "as Christ is the head of the church" (Ephesians 5:23), something of the divine splendour is reflected in our earthly relationships, and this reflection we should recognize and honour. The dignity that is here ascribed to the man lies, not in any capacities or qualities of his own, but in the office conferred on him by his marriage. The wife should see her husband clothed in this dignity. But for him it is a supreme responsibility. As the head, it is he who is responsible for his wife, for their marriage, and for their home. On him falls the care and protection of the family; he represents it to the outside world; he is its mainstay and comfort; he is the master of the house, who exhorts, punishes, helps, and comforts, and stands for it before God.[16]

The head of a home stands before God on behalf of his family and he lives before his family on behalf of God. This is the only headship God honors.

2

God's Reasons
for Servant Leadership

WRITTEN MORE THAN one hundred years ago, it has become the most famous love letter of our generation. When first read on Ken Burns's epic television series, *The Civil War*, the producer was unprepared for the response. Thousands of requests poured in for the transcript. Scores of newspapers reprinted the text. Framed plaques and needlepoint of the words filled craft store windows. Wedding presents carried quotations of the letter. Families began to research if they could be related to the couple responsible for the century-old correspondence.

The letter that caused such a stir was written by Major Sullivan Ballou to his wife, Sarah, a week before the first battle of Bull Run:

July 14, 1861
Camp Clark, Washington

My very dear Sarah,

The indications are very strong that we shall move in a few days—perhaps tomorrow. Lest I should not be able to write again, I feel impelled to write a few lines that may fall under your eye when I shall be no more. . . .

I have no misgivings about, or lack of confidence in the cause in which I am engaged, and my courage does not halt or falter. I know . . . how great a debt we owe to those who went before us through the blood and sufferings of the Revolution. And I am willing—perfectly willing . . . to help maintain this Government, and to pay that debt. . . .

Sarah my love for you is deathless, it seems to bind me with mighty cables that nothing but Omnipotence could break; and yet my love of Country comes over me like a strong wind and bears me unresistibly on with all these chains to the battle field.

The memories of the blissful moments I have spent with you come creeping over me, and I feel most gratified to God and to you that I have enjoyed them so long. And hard it is for me to give them up and burn to ashes the hopes of future years, when, God willing, we might still have lived and loved together, and seen our sons grown up to honorable manhood, around us. I have, I know, but few and small claims upon Divine Providence, but something whispers to me—perhaps it is the wafted prayer of my little Edgar, that I shall return to my loved ones unharmed. If I do not my dear Sarah, never forget how much I love you, and when my last breath escapes me on the battle field, it will whisper your name. Forgive my many faults, and the many pains I have caused you. How thoughtless and foolish I have often times been! How gladly would I wash out with my tears every little spot upon your happiness. . . .

But, O Sarah! if the dead can come back to this earth and flit unseen around those they loved, I shall always be near you; in the gladdest days and in the darkest nights . . . *always, always,* and if there be a soft breeze upon your cheek, it shall be my breath, as the cool air fans your throbbing temple, it shall be my spirit passing by. Sarah do not mourn me dead; think I am gone and wait for thee, for we shall meet again. . . .[1]

Major Ballou was killed at Bull Run.

Why the words of this Civil War soldier live beyond him is no mystery. Though the words are not theologically precise, they convey great strength and tenderness. There is no question about the courage of the author who was willing to die for his country. At the same time, he expresses affection so dear we want to blush for him. Such a man will be treasured in any age. He is so strong that he can afford to be tender. And the expense of his strength for the expression of affection becomes his wife's greatest treasure, the sure knowledge of her own preciousness.

Major Ballou's determination to use courage and love to give his wife strength and value reflects God's purposes for biblical headship. The servant/leader responsibilities God gives husbands have a redemptive intent. Jesus sacrificed so that his people could know their value to God (see Mark 10:45; 2 Cor. 8:9; Titus 2:14). Husbands who reflect Christ's headship use their authority as he did, seeking for their wives to know their preciousness to God.

To Glorify the Wife

Headship that honors Christ brings glory to women. Such husbanding enables a spouse to know God's care for her despite personal imperfections, circumstantial difficulties, and self-doubt. This redemptive purpose is apparent in Paul's comparison of a husband's care for his wife and Christ's care for his bride, the church:

> As Christ [the authoritative Lord of the universe] loved the church and gave himself up for her . . . by the washing with water through the word, and to present her to himself as a radiant church. . . . In this same way, husbands ought to love their wives.
>
> Ephesians 5:25–28

Our Lord submitted his life to glorifying his bride. To help her realize her eternal value, he purchased her beauty with his blood. He sacrificed to confirm her assurance of her preciousness to God.

Compare such a purpose to these words a Christian woman recently wrote about the head of her home:

> I hate him. I hate him because he made me feel worthless, inadequate—like a nonperson, a slave. I could never do anything that made him happy. I always came short of the mark. I was always desperately working to win his approval. I hate him for the crummy way he made me feel about myself. I don't know whether I will ever get over the hurt he caused in my life.

Instead of making his wife feel precious, this husband's headship made her feel worthless. We cannot excuse this wife's bitterness, but neither should we seek to justify versions of headship that, with the most self-serving selection of proof texts, ignores biblical purposes. Christ's love never makes us feel "crummy," "worthless," and "like a nonperson." The authority in this marriage was improperly expressed. It failed to confirm the divine value God purposes for his people. Such unbiblical headship is a form of robbery because it takes from a wife the knowledge of grace God intends for her to possess.

Robbing another of value sounds horrible, yet it is extremely common. Whether such robbery is deliberate or not, it is almost always the result of an insecurity that makes a husband try to establish his worth by controlling his wife. Some evil math in us seems to reason that when we have reduced another's sense of worth, then our own value increases.

My wife, Kathy, is one of the most competent, capable people I know. Her grades were far better than mine in school. She was repeatedly selected as the outstanding musician at her university. She possesses numerous academic and professional honors. Yet after we had been married only a short while, I realized that I was robbing her of her self-worth.

I made this discovery when our washer needed repair. I asked Kathy to call a repairman while I was at work. She agreed to do so but then did not. The next day she again agreed to call the repairman, but when I came home from work, she still had not called.

That evening, she confessed in tears that she did not feel capable of making the call. We both remember that night vividly. She remembers because the conversation now embarrasses her. I remember because it scared me.

I thought, *Kathy, what is wrong with us that after a year of being married to me, you—so capable and intelligent—think so little of yourself that you cannot make a phone call? How have I managed to reduce you to this? What have I done to you?*

I cannot say that answers came immediately to those questions—neither my actions nor my thinking were mature. What most helped me was an image that regularly flashed into my mind for months after our "washer" event. In my mind's eye I saw a framed print that used to hang in my grandmother's home. The picture shows a young man at the wheel of a great ship during a violent storm. Wind whips the sails into tattered sheets around the boy, and the waves crash about him. Yet despite the threat, the boy's face remains calm and confident. The reason is clear. Jesus is pictured standing behind the young pilot of the ship. The Savior's hand rests on the boy's shoulder, and the caption beneath the picture reads, "Jesus is my copilot." The words and the image communicate that in the presence of the Savior, our confidence grows.

Kathy's thought: Bryan now delights to tell people of a more recent time when our washing machine (not the same one) needed repair. I diagnosed the problem, drove to the repair shop, bought a replacement part, and installed it. It's hard for me to explain, even to myself, how insecure I was about small things earlier in our marriage. I could perform a flute recital or analyze a musical composition with no hesitation, but somehow being asked to handle something that affected both of us rattled my confidence. What if I made a bad decision? What if I messed up? I should have known that it wouldn't have mattered to him—to us. I should have trusted his love and respect to be unconditional. (Now, of course, I feel perfectly free to mess up—I know he's sweet on me!)

The opposite was happening in my relationship with my wife. My presence often made her self-confidence vanish. She felt like a capable driver until I was in the car. She never doubted her competence in social gatherings until I entered in the conversation. In a thousand ways (only some of which I recognized), I made my wife question her adequacy. I was robbing her of her self-worth. I had to reexamine myself in the light of Christ's love for the church. My headship should build up my wife, enabling her fully to sense the treasure that she is to me and to her Savior. She cannot easily know or reflect her worth to God if the husband he has provided diminishes her. She will not glorify God with the radiance he intends if her husband deprives her of glory.

The descriptions of Jesus' care for his spiritual bride, the church, provide important guidance for how Christian husbands should honor their wives. Paul says Jesus cleansed the church "by the washing with water through the word" (Eph. 5:26). This reference to the baptism that represents Christ's cleansing us from our sin holds important implications for husbands. The gospel of Christ's forgiveness should dominate our homes. This means that the message of the Bible should make a daily appearance in our homes. Family devotions, church participation, and personal encouragements are tools that God provides husbands to help communicate the joy of the gospel. In the premarital counseling I do, I have been struck by how often young women ask me to impress on their future husbands the importance of family devotions. These women know intuitively that the unity of their marriages, their personal self-esteem, and their joy in fulfilling God's purposes are furthered and secured by their husbands' commitment to God's Word.

Communicating Forgiveness

Of course, verbal commitment to the truths of God's forgiveness is a cruel sham if those truths are not lived out. A husband reassures loved ones of God's goodness and their significance when — as the head of the home — he reflects the reality of forgiving grace.

When Kathy and I were first married, we lived in a small, rented farmhouse. The roads from our home to our jobs were treacherous in the winter because our community did little to clear snow. We had one compact car between us — all we could afford. During an ice storm, Kathy slid off the road. Faced with a repair bill, a tow charge, and temporary difficulty getting to work, I had little mercy. I explained the need for greater care, I went into detail about how to turn *into* a skid to get control, and I reminded her that our finances could not handle such "accidents." Two days later, I put the car in a ditch.

Fortunately, the ice lasted a little longer and Kathy put the car in a ditch again. Unfortunately, so did I!

Our ice-driving experiences were an important reminder to me that everyone needs forgiveness. I think the Lord helped me into those ditches because the husband who realizes his need for mercy will most effectively communicate it.

The healing Kathy and I have experienced in our marriage (and seen in others) most often relates to forgiveness. A husband who grants forgiveness because he knows he also needs it shows his wife the grace that confirms his own status before God. As a result, forgiveness com-

Kathy's thought: So for anyone keeping score . . . Actually, our favorite ditch story of that first year was the day we were together in the car (Bryan was driving) traveling on a country road that was crowned so that rain would run off into the ditches. It was an icy day, and after negotiating a curve in the road, we continued to curve on the ice, and into the ditch we went. Fortunately, we were only about a quarter mile from the farm our landlord owned, so we walked onto his place, knocked on the door, and apologetically explained the situation and asked for his help. He very kindly got his tractor out of the barn and pulled the car out of the ditch. After we thanked him profusely, he drove away on his John Deere and we got into our Pinto, buckled our seat belts, started the engine, and promptly slid into the ditch on the other side of the road. Mutual humility, I think, was the lesson that winter.

municates the mutual preciousness of spouses, confirms the spiritual needs of both, and powerfully unites the couple in the knowledge that their weaknesses do not invalidate their love—or God's.

Confirming Beauty

Paul says Christ made the church radiant for himself (see Eph. 5:27). He promoted her beauty. I am *not* saying that we should equate personal value with physical beauty. Counselors tell us, however, that husbands who make wives question their appearance or who encourage their dowdiness often do so to control their wives. By making women question whether others will find them attractive, some men seek to isolate their wives and make them dependent on their spouses' approval. Other men make their wives feel inferior by openly admiring passing skirts or indulging in the airbrushed images of advertising and Internet fantasies.

Controlling anyone by demeaning them or by making them question their worth is abhorrent to God. God sent his Son to the cross to demonstrate to us that we are "dearly loved" (5:1). He commands us to say and do only what will build up one another in the knowledge of his care (see 4:29–32).

God intended marriage partners to be attractive to one another so that their physical union might strengthen the bond of their hearts. One way that we strengthen this bond is by affirming the physical and personality features we cherish. We husbands affirm this beauty by our loving words and by showing our wives that we desire them—with an affectionate hug as well as with the caring lovemaking the Bible honors (see Gen. 2:20–24; 1 Cor. 7:4–5; Eph. 5:31; Heb. 13:4). By provid-

Kathy's thought: I wish all husbands could understand how important it is to a woman to know she is lovely in the eyes of her husband. It isn't a vanity thing—it's a value thing. We long to know that the one we love finds us beautiful, inside and out, and that he cherishes us. Knowing that Bryan thinks I'm pretty makes me more confident. His appreciation of my ideas and abilities frees me to develop and use them. I consider my husband's affirmation of me to be one of the most precious gifts he could ever give me.

ing the loving support that makes a wife feel attractive, we encourage the beauty of appearance and soul that satisfies both spouses. The beauty we consistently cite, we increasingly see.

The Bible says Jesus made his bride, the church, radiant to him. Husbands should do the same with their brides. I love to shop for clothes with my wife (at least, in short spurts) not because my tastes are any good but because I enjoy seeing what makes her feel beautiful and being able to tell her so.

I realize many husbands dread this kind of shopping. It not only places them in the women's section of a department store, but it may seem to encourage purchases already having frightening effects on the family checking account. Yet a woman who is confident of her beauty (because her husband so affirms her) may feel less of a need for new frills to make her feel pretty—just as a secure man has less need to purchase the flashiest sports car or muscle shirt.

We diminish each other and our marriages when we do not communicate the ways in which we see beauty in our spouses. We praise God by rejoicing in the beauty he provides in our spouses.

Prioritizing Partnership

A husband further affirms his wife's value by obeying Scripture's command to give his union with his wife precedence over other family relationships, even that with his parents (see Eph. 5:31). This instruction does not annul lifetime responsibilities to honor parents but it does place priority on the marriage.

Advice columnists and daytime talk shows would run out of material if all men were to honor the Bible's hierarchy of relationships. The Bible says that a man shall "leave his father and his mother, and shall cleave unto [be united with] his wife" (Gen. 2:24 KJV). The traditional wedding vows capture the "leaving and cleaving" essence. The groom promises his bride to "forsake all others and cleave only unto her." This is more than a caution for in-laws to keep their distance. The couple promises to make their marriage relationship a higher priority than all others. The man who keeps this promise honors his wife and blesses his marriage.

When other relationships take priority over the marriage, pain follows. Everybody knows of families where a husband or wife lets a parent run (or ruin) their marriage. The woman who simply cannot say no to her mother's interference may be blamed for a marriage's trouble, but the man who will not exercise his authority to insist that the meddling stop is also ignoring Scripture. My wife and I know of a husband who, after years of suffocating in-law entanglement, required his wife's parents to sign a contract limiting their visits, criticisms, phone calls, and out-of-control giving of presents to their grandchildren. The pain involved in hammering out the agreement was intense, but prior to the contract the marriage was near rupture. The case is extreme, but the oneness God intended would never have occurred had the husband not taken charge.

Kathy's thought: It is good news to relate that, although the difficulties in this situation took years to resolve, the couple involved now enjoys a balanced and loving relationship with the wife's parents. Clarifying their marriage priorities with the in-laws strengthened the couple's relationship, and presenting a united front ultimately persuaded the in-laws of the wisdom of that choice.

A young man we know could not say no to his mother. She cooked him treats, bought him clothes, visited him every Sunday, and used him nearly daily as a handyman. This husband warded off his wife's pleas for attention and her warnings of the mother's manipulations with the excuse, "Mom needs me." So did his wife, and his failure to put her first clearly indicated her value. The young man now lives two doors from his mother, alone.

When the Bible commands that our relationship with our parents—which is of great importance—take a backseat to marriage, then the message is clear: no relationship should challenge the oneness of a husband and wife. A husband who confides more in his secretary or a work associate than in his wife damages the oneness God intends for his marriage.[2] A man more dependent on the approval of a close friend (male or female) than on that of his wife commits emotional adultery. A man married to a career, to a computer terminal, to a child's success, to a television screen, or to sporting interests more than to his spouse sins against her. When a husband treasures his wife as God intends, then no personal relationship or activity takes priority over the marriage bond.

Providing Care

By their care men indicate how they value their spouses. Paul says husbands ought to care for their wives as they do for their own bodies (see Eph. 5:28). The terms describing this care relate to physical provision as well as personal affection (see v. 29). Husbands should not use family resources selfishly. God mandates that our words and our goods should foster the well-being of our spouses.

Three decades ago a professor, who now teaches at Covenant Seminary, left the United States to direct an international ministry. His wife went with him, leaving a career she loved—teaching French at a prestigious girls' school. When the family returned to the United States twenty years later, her love for French had not diminished, but the family's savings had. There appeared to be no way for the wife to take the college courses needed to renew her teaching credentials.

The husband refused to deny his wife her love. By teaching an overload schedule for extra pay, taking temporary jobs, and avoiding all frills in the family budget, the husband sacrificed himself to give his wife the opportunity to teach again. She earned her degree but then, to the surprise of many, she chose to stay at home. Her husband's job responsibilities had become so pressing that she felt she needed to be home to support him. She still wants to teach, but she now sacrifices her desires for the benefit of the one who gave himself for her.

With so much sacrificing going on in this family, you might get the idea that theirs is a fairly morbid home. No way! Students and fellow faculty look forward to visiting this couple's home, because joy radiates from its every corner. Mutual sacrifice led by the head of the home breeds the deepest satisfactions love and life can offer.

At his wedding a husband vows, "All that I am I give to you, and all that I have I share with you." He promises to sustain, without reservation or concealment, the wife God provides. This promise does not prevent a man from delegating resources and responsibilities according to family members' respective interests, talents, and strengths; however, this division of labor should not be an excuse for hidden activities or hoarded treasures. A man who marries with the intention of withholding goods, accounts, or affection from his wife denies himself the greatest joys of the union God designed to build up both partners. A man who keeps secrets damages himself. Scripture wisely indicates that a man should care for his wife as he does himself. His wife's well-being is his own.

Cherishing Grace

Scripture's analogy of a man caring for his wife as he does his own body holds particular significance for how we handle marriage difficulties. A man remains faithful to his body even when it brings him pain. In fact, when his body signals pain, he typically gives it more attention. Everyone understands a husband who is faithful to a spouse when she brings him pleasure. But being faithful beyond pleasure makes sense only to those who cherish Christ's love and through it learn to value a spouse for who she is rather than what she offers.

Jesus sacrificed his body for us when we brought him not pleasure but heartache. This is the message of grace: God loved us when there was no human reason. He treasured us when we had no esteem for him (see Isa. 53:3; Mal. 3:17). To love your wife when her failures cause you hurt, to cherish her at the very moment you believe that someone else could satisfy you more, is to be Christ to her. Such love shows her that God's regard extends beyond good reasons and becomes the ultimate confirmation of her worth when all else screams her worthlessness.

None of the marriage hints above is more critical than the apostle's decree: "Husbands, love your wives" (Eph. 5:25). Paul attaches no condition to the command. He does not say, "Love your wives because they make you happy," or ". . . when they do what you want," or ". . . as long as they are beautiful to you." The command stands alone. To join it to any reason or cause would be contrary to the character of the God who issued the standard.

God loves us as a consequence of the relationship he has established with us, not because of any beauty we possess or any service we could offer. Nothing better communicates this grace than unconditional love. A husband who cherishes his wife to honor the divine covenant that binds them, rather than any good she does for him, honors both his God and his wife. Unconditional appreciation enables a spouse to experience more fully the glory of God's regard for her. Only when a wife knows this covenant love from her husband do the blessings and passions of marriage really have the opportunity to flourish and endure.

Some may feel this concept of headship having the purpose of bringing glory to a wife demeans women. The notion that women need men to build them up—as though women somehow are not capable in themselves—can perpetuate horrible stereotypes. Much of what is written in popular Christian literature about men "discipling their wives" and being considerate of their "hormones" is demeaning *and* wrong. The fact that God uses husbands to glorify wives should be balanced by the biblical understanding that neither men nor women (except those gifted for celibacy[3]) are complete without their spouses. God designed biblical headship not only to glorify the wife but also to make the husband all that God intends.

To Complete the Husband

What does God intend for husbands to be? Complete— emotionally whole and spiritually mature. But how will this completion come about? Paul says a man "will leave his father and mother and be united to his wife, and the two will become one flesh" (Eph. 5:31). This is more than a reference to the physical union in marriage. The language reflects the Lord's creation plan to make us whole persons. God created the wife to complement and complete the husband (see Gen. 2:20–24). Lest this sound demeaning of her, think of what it connotes for him. The man is ever incomplete, incapable of realizing the potential God intends for him, apart from his wife.

A Union Man

Because two people who marry are to be one, if either party damages, demoralizes, or degrades the other, then neither will be whole. Just as a basketball deflated on one side won't work, so a marriage with one side diminished deprives both persons of being what God desires. God has designed the similarities and differences of a man and woman in marriage to complement the spiritual growth of both. Neither can develop fully if either is denied his or her personal potential.

The man who thinks he will do "just fine," regardless of his unwillingness or inability to build up his wife, fools himself. By divine decree husbands and wives are united in mind, spirit, and body. God knits our marriages together and expects us to care for each other. If a man takes advantage of his spouse or robs her of some essential need, then he stunts his own growth as well as hers.

My wife and I once lived among students training for ministry. One evening we invited a couple to our apartment. We played a game that requires animated conversation but soon realized the wife was not fully participating. In fact, she was playing so miserably that the situation became embarrassing. She would hardly speak up.

When the awkwardness became intolerable, the husband finally explained to us why his wife was not speaking. He said she had recently embarrassed him in the company of others. As a result, they had agreed she should not speak in public unless he—the head of the home—granted her permission. They were serious about this! As a consequence, they did not win any of our games that night. There were other consequences too.

Some months after the game episode, the husband began to suffer severe depression and left the seminary. We have never heard from the couple again. Still, we have occasionally speculated on what this man did to himself. The Lord had provided him with a wonderful spouse. Yet by manipulation and intimidation, he had so weakened her that when he needed her support, she was incapable of helping him.

A man's headship should reflect Christ's redemptive activity on behalf of the church. The husband is an instrument and channel of God's goodness. As Christ enables each of us to use our gifts to bring glory to God, so proper headship enables a wife to bring glory to God. A man who makes his wife feel inadequate, incompetent, or incapable betrays his headship and his Savior. Not only does headship that demeans rob God of the glory he intends for a wife to bring him, it can also rob the husband of God's help in time of need. God designed the woman for her husband's support. If he has robbed her of the self-confidence to stand, she will be of little aid to him.

Husbands who admire (or are jealous for) the strong women they see in other men's marriages intuitively recognize that such wives enable their husbands to fulfill their greatest potential. What men with such a longing may not realize is that they play a large part in making their wives strong. The regard husbands give their wives often determines whether such strength of character will emerge in their own marriages.

A Real Man

Husbands require the support of wives. The more capable the wife, the better will be her aid. The man who understands this divine design for his own development delights to build up the woman who enables him to be what God wants. The regard a man gives his wife defines and develops him. So the best men build up their wives. Real men respect women. When this understanding fades in any culture, many suffer.

Church officials across this nation have expressed alarm that students training for ministry have had poor family models as a consequence of the breakdown of the American family. When these students become pastors, they know where the Bible tells how to deal with one's family, but actually living these words is another story. A childhood of pain can render an adult awkward, unsure of how to share feelings, incapable of showing affection, and unwilling to develop the vulnerability necessary to help others in pain.

A minister close to my family counts himself among those scarred by his childhood. Yet he recently wrote how—through his wife—God taught him to share more of himself with those committed to his care:

> So much of what I had to learn from my wife, after being in a home of constant tension, was simply what it meant to be caring and expressive. In so many ways my wife helped me find *me* when I got married. I did not know how to express

affection. I did not know how to express appreciation. I was out of touch with my emotions, having forgotten how to laugh or how to cry. Yet I was trying to be a minister of the gospel. I dread thinking of what my "ministry" would be if the Lord had not taught me to know and express care through the spouse he provided.

Of course being out of touch with one's own feelings is not a problem limited to pastors. The man who wrote the words above is not the first to realize that his wife had much to teach him about caring for others. I am by nature reserved. I have had to learn much from my wife about expressing affection, even to be able to relate to my children. Without her patiently drawing me out of myself over many years, I dread to consider the kind of father, husband, and pastor I would be. Even now I struggle to be as expressive as some of the people around me need. I still have much to learn, but I recognize that where I am, what I have done, and the joys I know in career, family, and ministry result directly from my wife helping me share more of myself with her and others.

A Godly Man

The influence a husband's headship has on his relationships should point to the spiritual implications of how a man expresses his authority. A husband who berates his wife and beats his children may claim the Bible's support. His actions, however, indicate he has denied the authority of God over his own life. Biblical headship requires constant examination of one's actions, attitudes, and priorities to see whether they conform to Scripture.

Deeper understanding of how headship affects one's relationship with God flows from reflection on how a wife's completion of her spouse affects his spiritual health. In a profound way, a wife not only helps a husband find himself, she helps him find God. The intimate is closely connected to the transcendent. The ability to express and experience human affection often opens the door to understanding God's love. If you cannot share your heart with others, then it is nearly impossible to have an intimate relationship with your Lord. The union of human hearts deepens our understanding of who God is by introducing us to the feelings, actions, and forgiveness God treasures. Thus headship that damages this union threatens our knowledge of God, just as the headship that promotes the union reveals him.

The early church father Tertullian wrote of the connection of Christ's love to the marriage relationship:

> How beautiful, then, the marriage of two Christians, two who are one in home, one in desire, one in the way of life they follow, one in the religion they practice. . . . Nothing divides them either in flesh or in spirit. . . . They pray together, they worship together, they fast together; instructing one another, encouraging one another, strengthening one another. Side by side they visit God's church and partake of God's banquet; side by side they face difficulties and persecution, share their consolations. They have no secrets from one another; they never shun each other's company; they never bring sorrow to each other's hearts. . . . [S]eeing this Christ rejoices. To such as these He gives His peace. Where there are two together, there also He is present.[4]

Through the analogies of human affection, we gain insight into the divine heart (see 1 John 4:20). By her love and patience my wife has made me more spiritually whole than I could be apart from her. I did not know the ways I failed to understand God until she opened doors in my heart that I did not realize existed. I have much still to learn from her. If I had continued to diminish her confidence, then I would never have learned to love deeply. I would have lost parts of myself. I would have lost the ability to fathom "how wide and long and high and deep is the love of Christ" (Eph. 3:18).

The intimate is often the path to understanding the transcendent. In the relationships God provides to help make us whole, we discover more of the pervading presence, care, and peace of our Savior. I praise God for the great grace of opening and maturing my heart through my wife's influence. I am thankful for the Word that reminds me that if I do not build her up, then I diminish myself. My sanctification, my wholeness before God, cannot be complete without my honoring Kathy. No wonder the apostle Paul says that the one who loves his wife loves himself (see 5:28–29, 31). By building up his wife, a man enriches his own life — and his own eternity.

As a husband uses his authority to nurture his wife, he experiences fulfillment. This truth is buried somewhere deep in all of us. By excavating our private attitudes toward those we know, we discover what Scripture attests: the men who respect their wives are whole people. Conversely, those who diminish or despirit their wives are often emotionally and relationally unhealthy on other fronts as well.

All probably know men in business, or even in the church, who are highly respected for their abilities on the job but whose home lives (hidden deep beneath the public facade that wives may also be desperate to protect) disclose a headship of authoritarian rule or self-interested abandonment. Families of such men bear the scars of their heads' stardom even though these men may prosper in their occupations for many years.

Such men substitute career success for family fulfillment. Sadly, people in the organizations such men lead also become mere cogs in the machinery of the head man's career. These men increasingly isolate themselves from feelings for others. They become puppets controlled by their own need for significance—a parody of success without satisfaction. Such men disappoint us when we meet them because we expect their success to have made them more complete and humane persons and, instead, we discover they are preoccupied with self-importance. Anticipation of worldly significance may lie behind our own drivenness because it is easy to believe that the respect of men equates with the regard of God.

Scripture warns against these false expectations by prioritizing family headship as the means of growing in godliness. If a man will not devote himself to biblical care for those for whom he is most responsible, he depletes the soil in which his own spirit must mature. The men who know the greatest rewards of this life—in terms of familial love, personal pride, and spiritual satisfaction—have invested themselves in wives whose support makes their husbands healthy and whole.

In the soft coal mines of southern Illinois, collapse of the mine shafts is a constant threat. For this reason the miners use huge bolts to anchor the ceiling of the coal shaft to solid rock above. The system works as long as the supporting rock is strong. But when the supporting rock is weak, the whole structure collapses. So when a man weakens the wife divinely designed for his support, then he endangers the human and spiritual potential of both partners in the marriage. God has better plans. He mandates the godly headship that strengthens and blesses both husband and wife.

3

GOD'S RESOURCES
FOR SERVANT LEADERSHIP

ALMOST A GENERATION ago, in a wonderful article entitled "Husbands, Forget the Heroics!" Karen Howe wrote:

> I once heard a Christian minister spend an hour talking on the biblical role of husbands and wives. He spent 59 minutes discussing the woman's need to submit and obey, and one minute summing up the husband's role. It was his grand finale: "Men, you must love your wives as Christ loves the church. What does that mean?" Dramatic pause. "It means you must be willing to die for her!" He sat down and colorful images raced through my mind of my husband leaping in front of an oncoming bull or offering himself to cannibals in my stead.

However, in view of the more likely challenges of diapers, dishes, and daily schedule juggling, Howe concluded, "Most women do not want their men to die for them. They want their men to live for them."[1]

The light sarcasm aside, Howe makes a worthy point. Saying that biblical headship involves using authority to serve God's redemptive purposes does not explain precisely what men should do. Grandiose statements about sacrifice can lead to daily inaction when such heroics seem unneeded. How are men to exercise headship daily?

The Bible offers no specific this-is-what-you-are-to-do instruction regarding doing the dishes, deciding when to move (or for whose job), or determining who drives, takes out the trash, or holds the remote control. Yet the resources Scripture gives men to help carry out their responsibilities tell what should govern a husband's considerations of both daily and eternal duties.

We might expect God to give husbands power, rules, and armaments for exercising authority. But the biblical instruction has nothing to do with physical power. The primary resource God supplies for headship is sacrifice—ours and his.

Self-Sacrifice

Robertson McQuilkin, a leader not only of his home but of the evangelical world, was, until 1990, president of Columbia Bible College and Seminary. He resigned from the presidency because his wife, Muriel, afflicted with Alzheimer's disease, needed his care.[2]

During his last two years as president, McQuilkin wrote that it was increasingly difficult to keep Muriel at home. When she was with him she was content, but without him she became distressed and panic-stricken. Though the walk from their home to the school was a mile round-trip, she often tried to follow him to the office. Seeking him over and over, she sometimes made that trip ten times a day. When he took her shoes off at night, McQuilkin found her feet bloodied from all the walking. Washing her feet prepared him for what most saw as an even more Christlike act—sacrificing his position to take care of her.

This is leadership by serving another—husbanding by humility, headship by sacrifice.

Leading by Godly Service

A Christian has the biblical responsibility to set the spiritual standards through which God will govern the family. What kind of authority is this? There is no quick way of saying it. Too often Christians try to summarize male headship in the home by simply saying that the husband has "the last word" or is the final authority in decision making. Be glad this abbreviation of responsibilities is not found in the phrases of Scripture because it can cause great damage. Such phraseology could mean that even if the wife

- hates the idea of moving to a distant town,
- doesn't want a particular home,
- thinks a child does not need another after-school activity,
- doesn't like a certain kind of lovemaking,
- disagrees with a husband's method of disciplining children, or
- believes an investment is unwise,

the husband automatically gets his wishes because he is the head of the home and has the final word. Such a concept does not exist in the Bible. While a husband may need to exercise final authority, he has no right to express it without consideration of his family's concerns.

The Bible takes care to direct a Christian man to use his authority for the benefit of his spouse and family. Biblical headship shifts the focus of husbanding from taking charge to taking responsibility. Being a godly husband is not so much asserting one's will as submitting one's prerogatives to the good of another.

Leading by Godly Nurture

In the same way a man feeds and cares for his own body, the apostle says the husband should provide for his wife (see Eph. 5:28–29). The King James Version uses the words *nourish* (to bring to maturity) and *cherish* (to foster with tender care) to describe this care that should parallel the way Christ loves the church.

These words include the concept of causing growth as well as expressing affection. As Christ gave himself to enable our spiritual growth, a husband has the responsibility of fostering spiritual growth in his wife. A husband should encourage his wife to develop her gifts and talents to bring maximum glory to God.

Christ nurtures the ability of each believer to honor God in two ways—by his past example and by his continuing aid. Jesus' compassion, patience, courage, holiness, and sacrifice show men what ideal husbands look like. His continuing intercession and provision of spiritual strength for us tells husbands how headship should marshal all available power and grace to provide for others' welfare even when ideals are not met.

By his prayer life, his patience, his meditation on God's Word, his integrity, his commitment to his church, his care for his family, and his love for and forgiveness of his wife, a husband fosters the personal and spiritual growth of his spouse. Giving of himself—as Christ did—to set a godly example for his family, a man leads his bride to honor God. Such giving of self may require much sacrifice.

Far into their elderly years a man in our church nurtured his wife's spiritual growth despite her resistance to his care. Because of some perceived slight by members of the church early in their marriage, the wife refused ever again to attend. Her resentment of the church grew as he remained faithful in attendance for decades. Some mornings he walked to church because she hid the car keys. One Sunday she cut the buttons off his suit to discourage his attendance. His example never wavered. He forgave her. He cared for her, and without speeches he demonstrated how much he valued his worship of the Savior.

She paid no attention until age made him an invalid and he could no longer walk. Even then his faith did not waver. Only then did his wife begin to consider what had kept his character and conduct so caring through the years of her resentment. From his bed the husband led his wife to an eternal relationship with God. Months later, a sudden illness caused her to precede him in death. The husband grieved but also rejoiced in the knowledge that he would soon be with her to share a relationship of deeper love than they had known in this life. A lifetime of sacrificial example bore eternal fruit because the head of this home nurtured the soul of his wife without regard for his own happiness or convenience.

This man's example should remind us that headship requires continuing effort if it is to nurture spiritual growth. Christ gave himself for us not just one time, but he continues to listen to our prayers, provide for our needs, forgive us, and love us. The Savior's continuing care causes us to grow in our ability to bring glory to God. So also a Christian husband should continue to help his spouse grow.

In the classic book *To Understand Each Other*, Paul Tournier writes of the rift that can develop in a home because the husband will not allow his wife to grow with him. Men accustomed to traditional home roles may presume that the concerns of a wife are mundane, simplistic, and without real consequence. She is concerned about Johnny's new tooth, the neighbors' latest fight, the new noise in the washer—or, of all things, uncooperative hair. Men consumed with workplace success may fail to see the importance of their wives' concerns for the security and well-being of the family reflected in these issues. Even if the wife is pursuing her own career, the husband may discover that while he discusses his job in terms of goals and tasks, she, on the other hand, speaks of her work from the perspective of personalities and tensions.[3]

Because they may be speaking on different planes (e.g., one communicating information, the other feelings), the husband can assume his wife is incapable of understanding his issues. As a result, he begins to withhold information from her, denying her access to his deepest concerns. Eventually he finds other people with whom to share his ideas, his troubles, and even his dreams. Slowly but inevitably the man cuts his wife out of his life. Later he will complain of his boredom with her. But it is a boredom for which he is responsible. He denied her the opportunity to grow with him because he had not the patience, the courage, or the compassion to broaden his horizons into her life or his vision with her insights.

A generation has passed since Tournier wrote. In that time the experiences of women inside and outside the home have changed dramatically, and his examples sound dated. However, the current popularity of gender research and books on how the sexes may relate differently to life caution us against disregarding Tournier. We may still be tempted to shut our spouses out of our deepest reflections because they do not process issues as we do. Our presumption should be that the companions God gave to complete us have contributions to make to our own growth. If we stifle those contributions or isolate ourselves from them, then we damage God's plan for our best life.

As two vines growing together become doubly strong, protecting and benefiting each other by their respective strengths, so God intends the marriage to support the development of each spouse. New gains in one support more growth in the other, enabling each to reach greater heights of spiritual maturity, character expansion, and godly honor. The biblical responsibilities of the head of a home require him to cherish and foster this growth that

Kathy's thought: When our children were little it was easy for me to worry about Bryan outgrowing me. He was finishing his Ph.D. and teaching at Covenant Seminary, meeting and working with brilliant and wonderful people, and learning all sorts of new ideas. I, on the other hand, was working with a four-year-old, a two-year-old, and a colicky infant. Keeping up with laundry, groceries, and housekeeping was almost more than I could handle. And I *was* concerned with Jordan's new tooth, the new noise in the washer, and uncooperative hair! (Our neighbors didn't fight, however.) My insecurities came bubbling to the top, and I worried that everything I wanted to talk about was silly and trivial and that I couldn't possibly understand anything in his world. We both had to adjust; he needed to hear what was on my heart and in our home, and I needed to listen to his dreams and ideas. We have learned a lot from one another—although there are many theological details and issues that are still way beyond me, and there are nuances of homemaking that my husband still doesn't get.

benefits each person and honors God. This purpose will be thwarted, however, if either person in the marriage ceases to grow—or is not allowed to grow.

When Kathy and I were first married, I was more concerned for my control than I was for her growth. I was not trying to be cruel but was simply attempting to fulfill my biblical responsibilities. I thought being the head of a home meant that I had to make all the decisions, no matter how small. I had to decide what we would eat, whom to visit, what Kathy should wear, when we would sleep, when to get up, what cereal to buy—it was exhausting. I was drowning in decisions. In taking over the life of two persons, I was struggling to keep my own head above water. I did not understand that my wife could not support me the way God designed if I gave her no opportunity to express herself. Thankfully, the Lord had my rescue and correction planned.

I spent a day trying to comfort a friend who had recently divorced. Despite the recentness of his separation, he had enough perspective to identify his major contribution to his marriage's failure. He said, "Bryan, not allowing my wife to grow was the unhealthiest thing I did to our marriage. It ruined us."

This was not an evil man. He was intelligent, honest, and faithful to his wife. Still, the constrictive nature of his nurture suffocated his wife. When she could stand to be stifled no more, she grew without him—and away from him.

As my friend described his dealings with his former wife, I recognized much of myself in him. I tried to learn what God was teaching me about leadership that fosters growth. But even when a man wants to encourage growth in his wife, he may not know how. Karen Howe offers insights from a woman's perspective:

> [Y]our wife has dreams and projects, too. Can you genuinely take an interest in her projects and sincerely rejoice with her when they prove successful? . . . What if she receives gifts from God's spirit that differ from your own—can you be glad for her and encourage her in their appropriate use? . . . Don't try to mold her, or suppress her; fulfill her. Honor her tastes and preferences as you honor your own, even if hers are decidedly different. . . . Paul urges Christian men to "nourish" their wives, as Christ nourishes and feeds His church. . . . This means . . . assessing her needs, physical and emotional, and trying to meet them. Could you accurately describe the areas where your wife is most in need of help?
>
> The burden of childrearing is a heavy one, and seems to fall most heavily upon wives. If your children are not doing well in school or are having difficulties emotionally, your wife probably feels frightened and guilty. Take leadership in this, find out what the problems are, reassure her, let her know you are assuming responsibility in this area.[4]

This list of "nourishment" suggestions can be lengthened and debated. What should not elude husbands is that nurture of wives is a leadership responsibility. Biblical headship demands that husbands encourage, stimulate, and even shield the gifts and growth of their wives.

Leading by Godly Character

Since Christ gave himself for the church to cleanse her from unholiness (see Eph. 5:26–27), a husband should give himself for his wife's progress in overcoming sin and drawing near to

God. Consideration of a wife's holiness may test a husband's character. For example, I have a tendency to recruit my wife to join in my anger. I want her to be angry along with me. If I am mad, I like the comfort of her assurances that I have been treated unfairly. It's always assuring when she agrees the problem is really the other person. However, my anger recruitment can lead my wife into bitterness because she sees only how I have been hurt. I have the opportunity to work through the problem with the other person. My wife does not. She can be left holding the bag of my dispute long after I have discarded it.

Realizing that my anger can leave my wife with damaging emotions, I now try to temper the way I express my difficulties with others. I want to shield her from having to choose between supporting me and honoring God with her feelings. My headship responsibilities need to govern how I seek her sympathy. I am responsible to remind both of us that God gives us no right to bitterness. I also must keep Kathy informed of the status of personal difficulties so her heart can process the stages of resolution with me. Being responsible in these ways helps mature me even as I seek to help her.

Kathy's thought: We realized the importance of finding this balance while we were in a small pastorate many years ago. A particular situation arose in which Bryan was being unfairly criticized by a man in the community. The criticism was especially hard for me to understand because I knew how hard my husband was working to resolve the issue. Bryan and I talked and talked, and my anger grew and grew. I'll never forget the day that Bryan came home and told me that he and the man had worked out the problem and "buried the hatchet." I remember that phrase because burying a hatchet was kind of what I had in mind, but in a different location! Bryan had the opportunity to work through the problem to a resolution, but I was left with a heart full of anger. I stewed about it for quite a while before the Lord got through my hardheadedness and made me see my sin. I want to know what's going on in my husband's life, and I want him to know my thoughts and struggles, but we have to take care to avoid simply getting one another revved up in ways that are inappropriate before the Lord and harmful to our hearts.

Other husbands may require different sacrifices to shield their wives from temptations. A woman who is particularly prone to worry or gossip or jealousy benefits from a husband who will express concerns in ways that do not engender inappropriate reactions. The man who objects to his wife getting counseling for serious problems because of his embarrassment over her need has abandoned his headship responsibilities for selfish pride.

Helping a wife mature in her relationship with God can be as straightforward as taking the lead in family prayer, Bible reading, and worship. Talking with a wife about the need to forgive helps bring healing for past hurts, especially if the husband acts forgiving toward her and others. Disciplining children with one's anger in control can help everyone understand that God's discipline does not deny his love. When a man appreciates the sensitivities of his wife in building family memories, in child rearing, in lovemaking, in home decorating, and so on, he communicates to her that he values how God has made her. When a husband believes (and says) his wife's tenderness enriches his life—rather than constraining his manhood—she will believe that God specially gifted her to nurture their family.

None of these practices, however, are more important than the husband's godliness. The heart of a wife longs for companionship and oneness with the man the Bible extols (see Gen. 2:24–25; Song of Sol. 2:3–13; Eph. 5:31). If a man's heart wanders from God, his wife's longings to be close to him will make his waywardness a threat to her holiness. The man tends to set the spiritual tone of the family. Wives who are spiritually mature (and personally undamaged) despite the godlessness of their husbands are rare. Though there are noteworthy exceptions, it is unusual for a woman to display godliness when she is married to a man disinterested in God.

Since all should honor God,[5] the head bears responsibility for encouraging family patterns of worship. Men cannot relegate faith concerns to their wives. In our society, spirituality is often thought to be effeminate. However, the man who recognizes the influence of his devotion on the spiritual health of his entire family will refuse to make his family's faith merely a feminine concern or responsibility.

The example the husband sets has eternal consequences. This means headship is more about controlling one's character than controlling one's wife. The man who is more concerned with how his wife should obey him than with how he should obey God fails the kindergarten of biblical headship.

Many families remain plagued by men who defend their self-serving bullying by mouthing a few Bible verses about women needing to submit. Such husbands not only ignore specific texts requiring caring male conduct (see Col. 3:19; 1 Peter 3:7) but also take out of context the Scriptures that describe headship.

In our marriages, as well as in the world, we all remain "Christ's ambassadors, as though God were making his appeal through us" (2 Cor. 5:20). To represent Jesus we must be willing to reflect his manner, suffer for his name, stand for his principles, and reflect his grace in our families. Nowhere does

Jesus say, "Follow my example of selfless love and sacrificial care except when you are home."

With great wisdom the Bible mandates no particular style, manner, or set of behaviors that alone qualify as biblical headship. In fact, there are probably as many legitimate expressions of headship as there are variations of personality. Biblical headship is simply a man's use of his God-given abilities and authority to ensure that love, justice, and mercy rule in his home, even when fostering such qualities requires his own sacrifice.[6]

In the rural town where I pastored for a number of years, a new Wal-Mart not only became the hub of retailing, it also became the social center of town. By hosting events for senior citizens as well as children, the store made itself "the place to be." Florence, an older woman in our church, practically made the store her second home. Shopping for "a few things I need" became a daily excuse to meet friends along the aisles, take grandchildren on shopping outings, or just share enough conversation with acquaintances to get up-to-date on the latest town happenings.

Florence's husband, Bill, was a retired carpenter who loved the outdoors. He enjoyed time at their nearby lake house, fishing and puttering. Each of them spent their days doing what they loved, though their love for each other was their deepest delight. That deep love showed itself when Florence could no longer drive herself to Wal-Mart. Now isolated from friends and family, she grieved when her daily excursions came to an end. But the grief did not last long.

Bill did not really understand his wife's enjoyment of Wal-Mart shopping nor did he desire to join her in it, but he soon recognized how much she missed it. One day he decided to forgo his time at the lake house. He drove Florence to Wal-Mart and stayed with her until she was ready to leave—which was not soon. On the many subsequent days that Bill took Florence to the store, he also took along a folding lawn chair. They would amble down the aisles together until Florence would strike up a conversation with a friend or stranger. Then Bill would unfold the chair and sit in the aisle until Florence was ready to proceed to the next conversation.

> **Kathy's thought:** No one ever showed us love in action better than this dear husband our whole church called "Grandpa Bill." He wasn't everyone's grandfather, of course, but he was the kind of man we all knew should be our family's patriarch.

As he sat in the aisle, silently beaming at his wife's enjoyment, Bill became the darling of our community. All knew his outdoor enjoyments. And all knew the quality of the man revealed in the sacrifice of his pleasures for hers. As a church leader in our community, Bill had taught many about the love of Jesus. His care for souls knew no societal boundaries. He was a friend to the destitute. Rebellious teens knew his care even when their parents had given up on them. Bill refused to recognize racial lines long before civil rights laws required the community to address its prejudices. Bill's leadership was beyond dispute because his character was beyond reproof. By giving himself for his wife in their later years, Bill was simply leading his family as he had led his life. His lawn chair was a symbol of the sacrifice that made his leadership so effective and noble.

Christ's Sacrifice

How can husbands live so? How can men sacrifice so? By recognizing that the ultimate resource God provides for Christian husbanding is Christ's sacrifice. It may seem disingenuous that Paul—so obviously speaking of the man/woman relationship in this key biblical passage that details standards for Christian marriage—says, "This is a profound mystery—but I am talking about Christ and the church" (Eph. 5:32). I am tempted to accuse Paul of joking here. "C'mon, Paul," I instinctively respond, "you know you are really talking more about earthly than spiritual relationships." Yet the more I look into my own heart, the more I see that the apostle meant his words. A husband's biblical love for his wife finds its root and resources in his knowledge of Christ's love.

Christ gave himself to pay the penalty for our sins. We have God's acceptance even when we fail to live up to his expectations. Those who trust in Jesus' provision are assured of the love of the King of the universe, regardless of their achievements. In God's eyes we are robed in the righteousness of his own Son, and thus the heavenly honor due Christ is ours. A man secure in this knowledge does not need to live at the expense of his spouse, seeking affirmation of his worth by the service he can demand of her.

If a husband is not secure in his relationship with his Savior—if a man needs to have control over another to have some confidence in himself—then he cannot love as God requires. Christ's love is our relational fuel. If our spiritual lives are running on empty, then we will suck energy from the life of our marriages. Men who confirm their manhood by the psychological, physical, or sexual control of their spouses actually reveal insecurities of the soul that leech personal esteem from the misery of others. Until the certainty of God's approval fills the wells of self-esteem in a man's heart, he will always be tempted to drain life from others.

Recently I was summoned to another town to try to help restore the relationship of an estranged couple. On the way from the airport the husband told me how much he loved his wife and how desperate he was for her to return home. Later that evening his wife picked us up in the family car to drive to a restaurant. There we had planned to begin our discussions. They never occurred.

On the way to dinner the husband could not restrain comments on the wife's driving, the shoddy car maintenance, and the route she had chosen to the restaurant. By the time we arrived, the husband had his wife so flustered that she was too nervous to eat.

From the backseat I watched as the man, who hours before had told me how much he loved his wife, now tried to control her by magnifying her self-doubt. This was not love; it was a cruel and selfish power grab. He was so desperate for his wife's return that he was willing to destroy her self-confidence to make her dependent on him.

The man's friends, family, and boss had urged him to try to mend the broken marriage. It became more and more apparent that he was seeking reconciliation because he needed their approval. My pastoral task over the next two days was to help the man understand God's grace—the only power that could release him from the insecurities that made him need his wife's dependence. Only through growing confidence in the unconditional love of his Savior has this husband begun to take baby steps in supporting his wife for her sake rather than his own.

We will have no ability to serve each other as God requires if we are not sure of our standing in Christ. Through confidence in their eternal standing, men find the strength to make earthly decisions that require sacrifice for the good of others. Christ alone provides the security men require to head their homes as God desires. When a man has no questions of his ultimate worth, he can rightly weigh his family's good against his need to accept a transfer, seek political office, or win an argument.

Great Christian leadership always flows from meditation on the Savior's great love. Six years after resigning his high-profile position to care for his wife, Robertson McQuilkin wrote of what had maintained him through the drain and pain of caring for his stricken wife:

> "How do you do it? What are your resources?" asked the host on the television show *Day of Discovery.* I hadn't thought about it, but since then I have. Praise helps. Right now, I think my life must be happier than 95 percent of the people on planet earth. Muriel's a joy to me, and life is good to both of us, in different ways. But I'm thinking of something more basic than "counting your blessings."
>
> By 1992, the blows of life had left me numb—my dearest slipping from me, my eldest son snatched away in a tragic accident, my life's work abandoned at its peak. I didn't hold it against God, but my faith could better be described as resignation. The joy had drained away, the passion in my love for God had frozen over. I was in trouble. . . .
>
> Of course, the passion of his [Christ's] love for me had never cooled. Even in my darkest hours when I felt my grip slipping and was in danger of sliding into the abyss of doubt, what always caught and held me was the vision of God's best loved, pinioned in my place. . . .
>
> Then I remembered the secret I had learned in younger days—going to a mountain hideaway to be alone with God. There, though it was slow in coming, I was able to break free

from preoccupation with my troubles and concentrate on Jesus. When that happened, I relearned what God had taught me more than once before: the heavy heart lifts on wings of praise.[7]

Praising God for the "pinioned" Savior renewed this great leader's heart and headship commitments. The grace that provides security beyond our achievements also provides strength beyond our abilities. The ultimate resource we have to enable us to love as Christ requires is Christ's love for us. That is why, when he gives marriage instructions, Paul even more carefully spells out the assurance we have of God's love for us. When we rest in his love, we can reflect it. The degree of confidence we have in his care will largely determine the measure of selflessness we can express.

Husbands—and wives—I know I have not in these few pages answered all of your questions about Christian headship. Most of us have much to learn about this biblical imperative, but the path to understanding remains graciously plain. If a husband's constant effort, consistent motivation, and deep desire is to love as he is confident Jesus loves him, then that man's leadership choices are neither as obscure nor as harsh as the world tempts us to imagine.

When Robertson McQuilkin first wrote of his decision to resign his position to care for his wife, he reported that he was startled by the response he received. Husbands and wives who heard the account renewed their marriage vows; pastors told the story to their congregations; young people attested to a rekindled desire for a marriage commitment they had previously mocked.

McQuilkin said, "It was a mystery to me [why so many were responding so passionately to his care for his wife] until a distinguished oncologist, who lives constantly with dying people, told me, 'Almost all women stand by their men; very few men stand by their women.'"[8]

How curious that in becoming a servant to his wife, this man became a leader of men and women across the world. There is really no mystery in this. McQuilkin's actions reflect the heart of the gospel. We lead most clearly, most effectively, most authoritatively, and most like Christ when we live most sacrificially.

This husband became a leader to the most people when he applied his gifts, talents, authority, and calling to the care of a loved one. God calls us to believe that, in a similar way, each man becomes a leader in his family when he exercises his gifts, abilities, and authority in the service of his loved ones. The Lord who submitted himself to the cross on our behalf calls husbands to be no less submissive to his will by being a servant/leader in their home. There the husband takes the lead in dying to self to fulfill Christ's calling and reflect his glory. The head of the home is Christ's representative to the family. Thus he orders his life with the understanding that the path of Christian leadership is always the way of the cross.

THE SACRIFICIAL WIFE

Noble Love

Wives, submit to your husbands as to the Lord. For the husband is the head of the wife as Christ is the head of the church, his body, of which he is the Savior. Now as the church submits to Christ, so also wives should submit to their husbands in everything.

Ephesians 5:22–24

I WAS IN MY first days as a seminary professor. He was in his last days as a seminary president. Still, though his days on earth were nearing completion, Dr. Robert G. Rayburn, the founding president of Covenant Theological Seminary, invited Kathy and me to dinner. Though it was his custom to welcome new professors in this way, the cancer Dr. Rayburn was fighting made this invitation particularly meaningful to us—and difficult for him.

Seated at the head of the table, President Rayburn remained the unquestioned authority in the house despite the weakening of his body. His bearing was almost regal, though his hands quivered as he served our meal. His habit at dinners was to serve his guests and his wife from a side table. Now the cancer made this service painful and awkward. The custom continued only because Mrs. Rayburn had rolled a cart with serving dishes next to Dr. Rayburn's chair.

He served us because she helped him do so. This was only the beginning of her service. Throughout the evening we watched in silent admiration as she preserved his dignity through deft and subtle gestures. The steadied hand, the occasionally completed sentence, the slight movement of an article of furniture that kept him from tripping—all enabled him to serve us and preserve his honor, while they ennobled her. The dignity she provided him became her own, since only by her aid did he fulfill his purposes.

> **Kathy's thought:** This too was love in action. No one at the table that evening would have been surprised or thought any less of either of them if Mrs. Rayburn had served the meal, rather than enabling her husband to do so. Yet she acted in such a way as to honor him as he served us.

That evening is forever etched in our minds as a poignant display of the relationships the Bible promotes. The head of the home used his authority to serve others, including his wife. In turn, the wife used her gifts to support that authority, and so her efforts served both him and those he served. As each gave for the good of the other, each shared in the other's dignity.

What does God expect of women to promote this mutual dignity? The complexities of our age require us to examine

Scripture with extreme care to make sure answers to this question are not derived merely from personal opinion. As husbands were challenged to remember their biblical responsibilities in the first part of this book, we need to examine God's instructions for wives.

The key principle we will see is that God wants all in the home to dispense his grace. When we understand how he can use each of us to share his love, then our responsibilities become blessings rather than burdens. By sharing ourselves as God intends, each family member finds unequaled meaning, purpose, and security. In families where such love flourishes, joy thrives and the dignity of each person grows.

4

A WOMAN'S RESPONSIBILITY

The Completion of Another

WHEN FERGIE MARRIED Prince Andrew, we mar-
veled at the days of pageantry surrounding the royal
English wedding, but the moment most replayed on televi-
sions around the world came as they said their vows. Fergie
was supposed to say, "I promise to love, honor, and *obey*. . . ."
She did say the phrase, but with a sideways glance at the
prince that said much more. Her smirk clearly articulated the
new duchess's thought: "You gotta be kidding. Nobody really
believes those old-fashioned words about wifely submission
anymore, and *you* had better not!"

She repeated the vows, but with a toss of her head Fergie as
clearly tossed away the content of those words. In hindsight,
her careless lip service to traditions she did not really intend

to honor became a sad metaphor for the royal marriage. But it is not merely royalty to whom the metaphor applies.

If we listen past the lip service we pay to the official positions of our churches, political parties, or family traditions, we also hear questions about the responsibilities of women in marriage. A campus minister at Vanderbilt University put it this way: "It does not matter whether the intelligent women on this campus are liberal feminists or conservative traditionalists; if you can get them to talk honestly about their deepest concerns, most will say that they constantly wonder if their personal choices are correct. Deep down they are desperate for a credible authority to help them decide what women are supposed to be."[1]

Sadly, our churches have not been able to settle the issue. For example, some church leaders urge women to leave abusive husbands. Others tell women to submit to husbands guilty of the same offenses, saying the abuse is a result of wives not being submissive enough. I hear confusion among my own relatives as women, deeply desirous of honoring Scripture, have cried out in emotional exhaustion and spiritual agony, "I know that the Bible says to submit but I can't continue to live this way. I have tried but I can't keep on. I just can't."

From palaces to campuses to churches to our homes, the questions echo: how really is a wife supposed to love, honor, and obey? Flip answers that do not consider the challenges of our times, the dignity of each person, and the authority of God's Word will not suffice.

So what is a Christian wife to do? The plain answer of Scripture is that a Christian wife is to submit. The Bible says, "Wives, submit to your husbands as to the Lord" (Eph. 5:22).[2] However, neither mouthing ancient dogma nor mindlessly shouting "Submit" at modern women will settle today's concerns. The true duty, dignity, and beauty God intends for wives unfolds only as we consider the significance of his intentions for them.

Submission Does Not Mean Nothing

We can neither ignore nor trivialize God's desire for women to submit to their husbands. The apostle Paul first uses a compelling expression and a clarifying example to demonstrate that a wife's submission has both earthly and eternal significance. Then the apostle extends the responsibility so far as to make it impossible to circumvent or dismiss it.

The Scope of the Apostle's Words

A COMPELLING EXPRESSION

Despite our culture's aversion to anybody submitting to anybody, we cannot sidestep Paul's encompassing words about wives' submission. He underscores the importance of the responsibility with a compelling expression. Wives are to submit to their husbands "as to the Lord" (Eph. 5:22). This phrasing does not mean that a wife should treat her husband as though he were God. We are not to make idols of anything or anyone. Rather, the words indicate that a woman's submission is motivated not so much by a husband's deserving it as by love for God's purposes. She renders the service the Bible requires as to God himself (with all appropriate devotion and joy), rather than measuring what she owes another human (whose failings may make her service seem unfair and onerous). As a woman submits to her husband, she looks over his shoulder to see the Lord who is saying, "You are ultimately doing this not for him but for me."

Submission motivated by love for the Savior who suffered for us can help a woman whose friends or inclinations encourage her to base her actions (or nonactions) on her husband's worthiness. Such false encouragers whisper, "Why should you serve a person like that if he treats you so poorly or is so unappealing?"

The Bible, on the contrary, encourages us to serve one another not because others deserve our service but because God deserves our devotion. (For a more extended discussion on responding biblically to a spouse undeserving of respect or guilty of abuse, see chapter 6.) The fact that God is using us for his purposes explains the necessity of our service, provides the motive for our obedience, and underscores the importance of both.

For more than thirty years after she committed herself to living for her Savior, the wife of a police captain in our town prayed for her husband. In the early years of her marriage, she confesses, she tried to preach him into a commitment to Christ. He responded to none of her arguments or ploys. She ultimately resolved merely to love him despite his grizzled manner and occasional mocking of her faith.

For many years she cared for her husband with the "gentle and quiet spirit" that the apostle Peter advises for the wives of non-Christians (1 Peter 3:4). Finally the hardened police captain did respond. Now he too serves the Savior.

Once I asked this wife what had kept her living sacrificially for her husband. Unspoken between us was also the question of how she had continued to live for his good when he had made her life painful. She responded simply, "When I became a Christian, I fell in love with Jesus. My love for him made me want to do what he wanted for my husband."

When a wife submits to her husband "as to the Lord," heaven's purposes compel her, even when human reasons or rewards seem remote. Through this heavenly perspective, the apostle makes it clear that a wife's responsibility is not removed because her husband is difficult. Wives are to prioritize their lives so as to serve the purposes God has for their husbands.

A CLARIFYING EXAMPLE

The apostle supplies an *example* to clarify the nature of a wife's submission to her husband. He says that as the church submits to Christ, so wives should submit to their husbands (see Eph. 5:24). As the church could not fulfill its purposes without submitting to the will of the Lord, women cannot fulfill God's intentions if they do not submit to their husbands. A woman disobeys God when she ignores, undermines, or counters the proper authority of her husband. At the same time, the apostle's example frees the wife from submission to ungodly demands since the church's submission to Christ never includes participation in evil.

Churches sometimes err by teaching women they must do whatever a husband wants regardless of its moral consequences. Because a wife is to submit to her husband as the church submits to Christ, she remains spiritually responsible for her actions. A husband has no right to require of his wife what is contrary to God, and she has no obligation to obey what forces her, him, or their family against God's will. Submission is an act of worship whose primary purpose is to honor God. The requirement to submit to one's husband never takes precedence over the requirement to submit to

God. God requires respectful but firm resistance if a spouse demands disobedience to God.

THE COMPREHENSIVE EXTENT

Finally, lest we assume these standards apply only to some narrow slice of life, the apostle states the *comprehensive extent* of his instruction. He says that "wives should submit to their husbands *in everything*" (Eph. 5:24, italics mine). As already noted, these words do not mean that women should submit to ungodly demands. However, the apostle makes it clear that submission responsibilities do not expire after church. They do not apply only to a certain category of decisions or only when the submission is easy. The Bible requires a wife to respect the authority God gives her husband in every dimension of their relationship (see vv. 24, 33).

When the careers of a husband and wife conflict, when dramatically different views about child rearing or money management divide couples, and when our culture says no one's will should have priority over another's, it may be extremely difficult for a woman to submit to the authority of her husband. The Bible does not belittle this difficulty. Neither does it annul a husband's authority. Should our minds object that the Bible's writers simply did not anticipate the nature of modern society, we should remember that God gave these instructions when the sophisticates of Greek and Roman society were also blurring distinctions of men and women.

When the home is functioning biblically, the husband will consult and honor his wife's input into family decisions. Caring compromise characterizes the home where husband and wife are seeking to honor God and each other. The Bible tells husbands to be considerate of their wives and to treat them with *respect*—the same word used to describe how we are to honor kings.[3] However, even when this regard is not given, the Bible instructs wives to respect their husbands' decisions that do not demand disobedience to God. When a wife loses respect for her husband, the marriage quickly weakens.

Early in our marriage Kathy enjoyed spending summer evenings with friends gathered on a neighbor's porch swing. The evenings were full of laughter and teasing, but after a few weeks Kathy stopped joining the others. The wives delighted in exchanging tales of the stupidities and eccentricities of their mates. Kathy said she felt increasingly out of place (even though her husband's foibles could have provided her a rich supply of anecdotes) because she did not feel she could honor Scripture and participate in the ridicule. Kathy said, "I can't make fun of you in someone else's home and respect you in our home."

My wife's honesty about how difficult it is to maintain respect for a spouse in one arena of life when it does not exist in another helps explain the apostle's encompassing words. He says there should be no aspect of life and no time of life when a woman refuses to submit to the *biblical* authority of her husband. So long as he is not using his authority to impose something contrary to God's Word, the wife is to

> **Kathy's thought:** It has become a common practice in today's society to make fun of one's husband. Look at almost any current sitcom, and you see a beautiful, capable woman matched with a sweet but slightly dull-witted man. The joke's on him, in most cases. His hair, his weight, his housekeeping abilities, his hobbies—all are fair targets for the quick-witted female. Although I appreciate the woman being portrayed as smart and funny, it breaks my heart that her regard comes so often at the expense of her husband. One of the deepest sources of joy in my heart is the respect I have for Bryan. He is a man of great integrity and godliness. I delight in his dreams and goals and accomplishments. It is tempting, at times, to join in the jokes, because who doesn't like to come across as witty? It's kind of fun to get a laugh from my friends. But if my heart's desire is for my husband to be glorifying the Lord by his thoughts and words and life, what do I gain by diminishing him?

submit to her husband "in everything." These words are truly *comprehensive*!

The Scope of Scripture's Witness

Though the apostle Paul's instruction is comprehensive, we might choose to disregard his words if they seemed to be exceptional. If these words about a wife's submission were merely an isolated reference in an obscure verse, then it might be better to downplay what seems so sure to offend so many. But the requirement for wives to submit to husbands is not limited to one obscure verse.

At least three times in the Ephesians passage, Paul instructs wives to subject themselves to their husbands' authority (Eph. 5:22–24, 33). The apostle repeats this instruction in five of his epistles — 1 Corinthians, Ephesians, Colossians, 1 Timothy, and Titus. Such teaching is not Paul's alone. The apostle Peter also tells wives, "Be submissive to your husbands so that, if any of them do not believe the word, they may be won over without words by the behavior of their wives" (1 Peter 3:1).

The New Testament writers assure readers that these marriage standards are not unique to the apostolic age. Peter commends the submission of wives to the authority of their husbands in his era because "the holy women of the past who put their hope in God . . . were submissive to their own husbands" (v. 5). Peter ties the requirement of a submissive spirit to Israel's earliest history. He encourages wives to be "like Sarah" who two thousand years previously had "obeyed Abraham and called him her master" (v. 6). Paul goes back even farther by relating his instruction to the husband/wife relationships established at creation (see 1 Cor. 11:7–10; Eph. 5:31).

Scripture's instruction for wives to submit to their husbands is sweeping and consistent. Far from being limited to an obscure reference, the concept appears across Paul's letters, reappears in other New Testament writings, finds precedent in Israel's origins, and receives its design at humanity's creation.

Submission Does Mean Something

We cannot sweep aside instruction that receives such frequent and far-reaching attention in God's Word. But we still have to know what submission means. The original word is a combination of Greek terms that in rough translation would mean "to arrange under."[4] In the "street talk" of ancient times submission conveyed only the idea of subservience, but that is *not* what the Bible means.

The biblical contexts convince commentators to interpret submission as "a disposition to yield," "voluntary yielding in love," or "not to exercise authority over."[5] To these technical ideas can be added the colloquial commentary that biblical submission means that "a wife should follow her husband's lead, but it does not mean that she should be her husband's shadow."[6] Though the specific definitions vary a little, submission includes actions, since it involves *obedience* (see 1 Peter 3:5–6),[7] and it includes attitudes, since it involves *respect* (see Eph. 5:33). Such word studies help, but we do not really know what God expects of wives until we examine the contexts in which the apostles use the term *submit*.

To Complete Another

We understand what biblical submission means by the purposes it fulfills. Paul discloses these purposes using words from Genesis: "For this reason a man will leave his father and mother and be united to his wife, and the two will become one flesh" (Eph. 5:31–32). These ancient words remind us that marriage commits two people to a union that forms their mutual completeness. A marriage will never fulfill God's purposes if either person abandons care for the fulfillment of the other. Thus a wife's responsibility involves pouring herself into the completion of her husband.

Sacrificing one's self to make a relationship (and those in it) whole defines the essence of biblical submission. The subtleties and complexities of any marriage make it impossible to simplify such submission to a few rules for home etiquette. Paul says the ways in which two become one is "a profound mystery." It is past our explaining (and yet so obvious to us) that God has made those of us not gifted for celibacy[8] never quite whole — in personal development or spiritual maturity — without the one who completes us in marital oneness.

The connection of personal wholeness to marital completion becomes evident as we look at another individual (or even at ourselves) after a few years of marriage. We observe that the person has so matured, so leveled out, or become so much less self-absorbed since marrying so and so. At least that is what we see if the marriage is functioning well. If the marriage is going poorly, we typically recognize that the individual's self-absorption, immaturity, or character flaws are even more prominent.

If you are dishonest with the one God intends to know you most intimately and mature you most profoundly, you sacrifice spiritual development that is needed to safeguard you in other areas of life. A person engaged in an extramarital affair not only damages the oneness of the marriage but stunts his or her own character development. Lack of consideration for one's spouse (in habits, conversation, or faithfulness) almost always creates an individual whom others see as self-centered and ruthless. Seeking their own advantage, neighbors and co-workers may laugh at the jokes and cater to the interests of such an individual, but they know better than to trust a person who does not honor the trust of marriage.

When the oneness that God intends for marriage does not occur, we become less than whole. The abuse or neglect of that union damages both persons (see Gen. 2:20–24; Eph. 5:31).

Knowledge of how our lives affect each other helps shape our understanding of the mutual responsibilities of marriage. To the husband Scripture gives authority for biblical headship designed to lead a family in godly paths. To the wife God commits supportive care of the husband so that he can carry out these duties. At creation God described these responsibilities. Eve was to be Adam's "helper"—"a help meet (i.e., suitable or compatible) for him" say the historic translations (see Gen. 2:18; 1 Cor. 11:8–9). Far from being demeaning, the "helper" term refers to God himself elsewhere in Scripture.[9] Thus the helper language reminds us that a wife fulfills heavenly purposes in her home.

God intends for each wife to complement her husband so that together they fulfill God's expectations for their lives more than either could separately. Each has responsibility for the other so that the family unit is whole and healthy before God. Elisabeth Elliot captures this purpose well:

> The first woman was made specifically for the first man, a helper, to meet, respond to, surrender to, and complement him. God made her *from* the man, out of his very bone, and then he brought her *to* the man. When Adam named Eve, he accepted responsibility to "husband" her—to provide for her, to cherish her, to protect her.[10]

Each of us bears God's image, but in a marriage we do not fulfill the potential of that image without the spousal oneness of God's design. The wife's complementary gifts help refine the spiritual character of her husband, even as God uses the man to lead all members of the family (including the wife) to honor Christ. The wife fulfills a redemptive purpose in the home, enabling each person more fully to know and be what the Savior desires. She does this by submitting herself in love to the good of another, and in doing so she reflects Christ's sacrifice. As his image bearer she becomes his chief representative to her spouse. Like her husband, the wife lives for another and thus represents Christ in and for the home.

A wife who offered herself for the completion of her home and husband surfaced in the confession of a friend who visited my family. My friend Steve came to see us when his family was in trouble—because of him.

When Steve was a child, his father intentionally drove Steve's psychologically fragile mother into insanity in order to have an uninterrupted affair with a neighbor. So horrible was Steve's childhood that he could not remember a single conversation with his parents. He could remember their fights outside his bedroom.

The trauma of his childhood was now reaching into Steve's own family. Without healthy family models, Steve confessed he did not know how to relate to his wife and children. That is why he came to observe our family. He said, "I must have new family memories to draw on so that I can love my family as I should."

What Steve did not tell us at the beginning of his visit was the event that had caused him to seek our help. That revelation came later.

Despite deeply loving his family, Steve struggled with a violent temper. A little more than a year prior to his visit, a particularly angry rage had scared even Steve. When he had calmed down, he promised his wife that if he ever lost his temper like that again, he would leave her and the children for their protection. Steve did not want to subject his family to the trauma of his youth.

In the year following his promise, little changed in Steve's behavior. The angry episodes continued.

Steve's wife never responded in kind to his rages and she never reminded him of his promise. She endured his anger for a year. Then on the anniversary of Steve's promise, he launched into another rage. This time his wife ran to the bedroom and wept uncontrollably.

Her unprecedented response sobered Steve. He sat on the bed beside her and asked, "Honey, what is it? You never let my fits upset you like this before." Then she reminded him of the promise.

"A year ago on this date," she said, "you told me that you would leave me and the children if you continued to lose your temper. When you made that promise, I knew that you could not control your anger. I didn't know what to do. So I went to our pastor. I told him what you had said and I asked what I should do. I didn't want to lose you. I don't want you to leave."

She continued, "The pastor told me that I could not change you—only God can do that—but that I could pray for you. So every day I have prayed for you. I have asked God to take away your temper and I have never reminded you of what you said. But you haven't changed. When you lost your temper today, a year after you made that horrible promise, I started to lose hope. I love you so much, but I don't know what to do anymore."

What she had already done is what changed Steve. Daily she had given herself for him in faithful prayer and care without resentment. By her sacrifice she had been as Christ to him, though Steve had been blind to her ministry. When he realized how long his wife had applied every ounce of her spiritual resources to helping him, his heart and pride broke. That is when he came to our family to learn how to honor the sacrifice of his wife.

The changes in Steve were not immediate, but they were definite and progressive. He matured into the kind of husband and father God desired him to be as a result of the support God designed and enabled his wife to give. God used her "gentle and quiet spirit" (1 Peter 3:4) to give Steve the resolve he needed to address the wounds of his past and to lead his family. He and his family are now more spiritually, relationally, and emotionally whole because his wife poured herself into the completion of her husband.

The specific actions to which God calls other wives may be quite different as they consider how they contribute to the completion of their husbands. Some may be called to greater sacrifice. Others may find that God will use a wife's favorite activity or special talent to encourage a husband. God did not make marriages with a cookie cutter, and the ways in which wives may support, complement, and complete their spouses are usually open to a lifetime of discovery. But the realization that Christ intends for each wife to represent him—to be his hands and heart—for her husband is the key discovery that revolutionizes women's perceptions of their purpose in marriage.

It is important to remember that the goal is helping a spouse be what *God* intends. A wife who is devoted to making a husband what *she* intends indicates that she does not love her husband for what he is but for what she wants to make him. A wife who marries with the intention of reforming her husband rarely loves him deeply. Instead, she delays giving her whole heart to him until after he reflects the perfection of her makeover. Thus she is forever deprived of oneness with her spouse as he is in the present. A reforming wife dedicates herself to making a man in her image; a biblical wife gives herself to God, allowing him to use her in developing his image in her husband. In this she also reflects and represents Christ.

To Honor Another

Scripture consistently articulates the attitudes required for a woman to support her spouse, but the actions required are never as completely described. God tells us to sacrifice for each other but he does not provide a grid of habits into which every couple must fit their lives. Nowhere does the Bible say who should take out the garbage or carry groceries from the car. There is a remarkable absence of prescriptions for the daily operations of marriage. Apparently the goal of wholeness for the family is more important than any set of behaviors for all couples to observe despite differing personalities, gifts, and circumstances. This means that merely confining women to stereotypical roles will not fulfill the Bible's mandates for wives.

The inappropriateness of limiting a wife's responsibilities to cultural expectations becomes obvious when we understand that submission also involves *exercising gifts for the glory of another.* Consider the balance of Paul's words to wives *and* husbands. The apostle directs husbands to use their headship as Christ did for the glory of his bride, the church (see Eph. 5:25–27). A husband must never abuse his authority so that he robs his wife of "radiance" (see v. 27). At the same time a wife is to submit so as not to rob her husband of "respect" (v. 33).

Discerning how wives should honor their husbands requires us to unroll the implications of Paul's comparison of marriage to the relationship of Christ and the church. The church does not honor Christ by suppressing the gifts God provides. Rather, God calls her to arrange all her energies and abilities under the grand purpose of glorifying the Savior. To do less would not be submission; it would be disobedience. For instance, the gifts of music God gives

> **Kathy's thought:** When we were first married, Bryan paid the bills and balanced the checkbook for the first several months, then suggested I take over. His thinking was that, should something happen to him, he wanted me to be able to handle the finances. I won't even describe the state of panic that put me in. Although I had taken care of my own money during college, my expenses were few and I had never paid much attention to those pesky bank statements. Balance a checkbook? Wasn't the bank always right? I agreed, however, and since then (despite Bryan having had plenty of occasions to rue the day he suggested it!) I have paid the bills and balanced the checkbook. I have also taken over arranging for our health, home, and auto insurance and have purchased our last two cars.
>
> I do these things not because I am gifted in these areas, nor do I enjoy them. In fact, I rather despise paying the bills and keeping the books. Yet I do these tasks with a perfectly willing
>
> *continues…*

the church are not to be suppressed but fully expressed in praising him. To mute the church's music would be to deny God his due glory. Such gifts must find their proper avenues, of course, but simply restraining the gifts would deny the wisdom of the God who gave them.

This line of thought reveals the wisdom of Paul's terminology. Biblical submission truly is an "arranging under" of one's resources and abilities for the glory of another.[11] Such submission is never an abdication of responsibility for another's

heart because, by my doing them, I free my husband to devote more of his time and efforts to preaching, teaching, and writing, which are his gifts and, I believe, important work to which the Lord has called him. I value my husband's trust in me to do a good job, and I am glad to support him by taking from him those things I am capable of doing. And in doing so I have become far more confident that I can deal with life's difficulties and complexities—the very thing Bryan wanted for me.

welfare, nor is it an abandonment of one's own gifts to fit a predetermined behavior mold. Biblical submission requires a woman always to explore how to use the unique gifts and abilities God has given her to make the glory of God's image most evident in her spouse and home.

Each wife must determine how she can best bring the glory of God into her marriage. Universal directives based on societal preferences are inappropriate. The Bible does not specify who drives the car, who pays the monthly bills, or how many hours outside of the home a spouse may work or play without crossing some definite threshold of marital correctness. In fact, the ideal wife of Proverbs 31 engages in a great range of domestic, charitable, and business activities. Still, the Bible commends this woman not because of her industry alone but because of the support and respect she brings her husband through her endeavors (see Prov. 31:11–12, 23, 28).

Neither accepting nor rejecting cultural norms guarantees we are honoring biblical priorities. The responsibilities of marriage must be weighed in the heart with conscientious self-examination. The husband must ask not only, *Am I leading my family to a better knowledge of God?* but also, *Is my leadership self-serving or sacrificial?* The wife must similarly ask not only, *Do my actions, words, and attitudes support my husband so as to enable him to lead my family to a better knowledge of God?* but also, *Have I truly in everything submitted my life to this highest priority?* These are questions that cannot be answered by merely traditional or habitual role assignments.

When a woman, or her spouse, determines that she will not use God's gifts for the good of the family, then God's plan for all is damaged. This truth is sadly evident in the marriage of distant friends of ours. The husband is a church leader who sits on a council that examines new pastoral candidates. He asks the same question of every new candidate: "Does your wife submit to you?" The man wants each potential pastor to prove to the council that he controls his family the way the official controls his own family. However, it would be tragic if candidates actually did answer as this official desires.

Over the years this man's friends have watched as his intelligent, once glowing and buoyant wife has become increasingly silent, sullen, and dowdy under his "headship." The more withdrawn she has become, the more obnoxious, belligerent, and accusing he has become with everyone in his path. The more she retreats from her gifts, the more his excesses assert themselves. He becomes more like himself and less like his Savior.

This wife is *not* to blame for her husband's faults, but his friends cannot help but see in him the consequences of the suppression of her gifts. Still, despite the obvious, *both* parties in this marriage claim the wife is biblically submitting to her husband. As proof, they point to their habits: she talks only when he allows, leaves the home only when he permits, and wears only what he approves. How sad! By limiting headship and submission to a certain set of preconceived behaviors, both have lost sight of the biblical priority of promoting God's glory in each other. Thus they have diminished each other.

I cannot prescribe the specific actions this wife should now take, nor do I pretend to know precisely what should have changed years ago. But what I wish she would hear is that submission does not mean abandoning another person to his faults or abandoning one's own gifts. As we express God's gifts while living in his purposes for us, Christ's glory shines in and through us—and his image becomes clearer in those whose lives we touch. Using all God provides both to support and to challenge respectfully those we love for their sake and for Christ's glory is consistent with the responsibilities of biblical submission—knowing that doing so may require courage and sacrifice.

To Mature Another

As we have seen, submission never requires a wife to sin. A woman also should not betray the reasons God placed her in the marriage by submitting to wrong authority. If a husband abuses his authority or abandons his spiritual obligations, then the duty of a wife committed to her husband's good is "no longer conscientiously to submit, but conscientiously to refuse to do so."[12] She must use the heart and brains God gave her along with the humility and courage he requires to promote the glory God intends for her husband. Again, the goal is not to get her way but to serve Christ's purposes for her husband. Writes Kent Hughes:

> The fact that a wife wants to honor her husband's leadership if possible does not mean she will sit in mute silence. Questioning his reasoning or acquainting him with his error is not evidence of a rebellious spirit, but rather of love. Refusing to support his moral folly is not sin. A Christian wife can stand with Christ against her husband with a humble, loving spirit which indicates her longing to honor his headship. The attitude is, of course, key.[13]

A woman married to a difficult man, of course, must confront perceived fault with great care, with great humility (for she may be wrong), and usually with great patience. The godly counsel of mature believers in the church is also indispensable in serious matters. I do not want to understate the pain that also may be involved in discerning how best to apply these biblical principles in a difficult marriage, nor the importance of applying them in a good marriage. It simply does not fulfill God's purposes to squelch all insights and instincts he has given a wife for her to help her husband. To confront error effectively, humbly, and correctly, a wife must believe God has given her gifts to benefit her husband and her marriage.[14] *Biblical submission ultimately is not the suppression of gifts but the full expression of them on behalf of another.*

Each of us brings to the marriage a unique personality, set of talents, and background that God intends to use to make our homes (and each person in them) better reflect the love and character of his Son. God does not want anyone to trash these gifts. By the interaction of each partner's unique gifts, God intends to mature each person according to a divine strategy that began functioning when he made these two persons one. However, we deny ourselves and each other the beauty of this design when we bottle up the gifts he wants expressed.

Of course there may be times that each person must temporarily set aside or more permanently direct his or her gifts for the marriage to function well. A spouse with a gift for socializing may need to curb the desire to respond to every party invitation out of regard for a shy mate. However, the spouse who is more sociable may also use this gift to teach the partner how to enjoy such occasions and deepen other relationships. My wife has provided this specific service to me, and as a result I am able to meet the expectations of my job in a way I could never have done without her influence.

More difficult compromises will need to be made when balancing careers, making moving plans, or deciding how best to care for children. Such decisions are less torturous when both spouses realize that neither has a right to disregard the gifts of the other and that compromise may be God's way of promoting the glory he intends for each spouse.

In the context of their culture, marriage, situation, personal interests, and individual gifts, a couple must determine how each person will fulfill his or her marriage responsibilities. Not using gifts would betray both the reason God gave the gifts and the requirement that they be used for another's good. This does not mean that a woman's gifts should determine what she does. Rather, God's call to support her husband should determine how she uses her gifts. God gives us gifts to help us fulfill our responsibilities, not to alter his designs for our relationships.

Some wives teach their husbands tenderness. Many add to their husbands' strengths. Each should discover the unique ways God has gifted her to make her husband know he is special in her eyes. As she does so, the man knows the deepest pleasures of God's care even when the rest of life is rotten. The woman who submits her life to God's purposes enables a man to know the glory of being treasured by God, even when the world seems to disregard him. A man who knows such glory because of the support of his wife will love and honor her more deeply than either of them could otherwise imagine.

I never want to ask my wife to be less than she is, for to do so would be to fault the way God has made her to provide the support I need. In the same regard, she should never deny the unique gifts God has given her to make me and our home more of what he intends. Love for our children and her spouse should keep her from the mere selfish exercise of her gifts. At the same time, this love should encourage her to find avenues for her talents and interests that enrich her life and, through her, enrich us all.

A friend recently sank into the classic male stereotype of refusing to ask directions after he had made a wrong turn to a vacation destination. His wife tried to help by grabbing a map from the glove compartment. She quickly spotted the road missed and began to give directions to get the family back on course—only to be interrupted by a teenage son in the backseat. "Hey, Mom, you can't tell Dad what to do," he said. "Remember what the Bible says: 'Wives are to suppress.'"

The mother quickly reminded her child that the Bible also says, "Children, honor your father *and* mother," and that the word his chauvinistic little mind was searching for was "submit." There was some humor in the situation, but also sadness. Already in this young man's thought, the biblical concept of submission had become synonymous with suppression. He had confused the exercise of a wife's abilities for the benefit of another with the repression of her knowledge despite the needs of another. Though these would seem to be concepts so opposed that they could scarcely be compared, such confusion regularly occurs in our culture, churches, and homes. Clarity comes when we consider the goodness God intends to promote through wives who meet their biblical responsibilities—and the dignity that is theirs as a result.

5

A Woman's Dignity

The Care of Another

I THOUGHT THAT I had spoken so carefully in the conference. I had spelled out the authority Scripture identifies for husbands as well as emphasizing their duty to use that authority selflessly. I said husbands were to love their wives as Christ loved the church. I reminded men never to use their position for personal advantage, passivity, or bullying. Later I spoke to wives about their need to submit, not as meek and mindless mice but by making full use of their gifts for Christlike support of their husbands. I meant to encourage, but for at least one woman my words were deeply wounding.

She stood on the periphery of the group of people that came to ask questions after my talk. She waited until the rest of the crowd had dispersed. Then she stepped forward.

Well dressed and confident in bearing, she exuded profes-
sionalism. She was articulate and kept her voice level, but
there was no mistaking her frustration. With her eyes fixed on
mine, she said, "Why is it you cannot see that by telling wives
they must submit their gifts to the support of their husbands,
you make women second class? I don't care how nicely you
state it and how kind you are trying to be. Once you make
women subservient to men, you devalue us and perpetuate
our oppression. Somebody must tell you that when you give
these talks, you rob women of the dignity God gives them."

I respect her concern and know that she speaks for many
other women. In an age of feminism, spousal abuse, two-income
households, equal opportunity laws, and gender-neutral political
agendas, it is hard to accept any words—even those of Scripture—that appear to demean women. As a husband and father
of daughters, I too find detestable any perspective that devalues
the worth of women. My concern toward such ideas is not merely
a result of family sentiment but a consequence of the biblical
teaching that each person loved by God is infinitely precious to
him. There is no difference in the value God places on individuals. He gave his Son to die on the cross to rescue each of us from
an eternity without him.[1]

But if God values each person the same, how can the Bible
teach that a wife should submit to her husband? The answer
resides in understanding: (1) the requirements of submission
are not limited to women, and (2) the requirements of submission do not change the value of individuals even when
their duties vary.

In heaven's accounting, persons are not valued according
to the level of authority they possess but according to God's
infinite, equal, and unconditional love. Our purposes vary but

our value does not. For example, an elder with authority in a local church is not of more value to God than the newest child member; a mom raising a daughter who becomes our nation's president is not less important than her child, for heaven's purposes. Their duties vary, and God has different expectations for how each of them should express their differing gifts, but neither is less significant. In fact, the Bible says, "Those parts of the body [i.e., the church] that seem to be weaker are indispensable. . . . God has combined the members of the body and has given greater honor to the parts that lacked it, so that there should be no division in the body" (1 Cor. 12:22, 24–25). Precisely because God has varied his design for individuals, each person has special dignity. Eternal purposes, not earthly position, indicate why each person is of equal importance to God.

The Esteem of a Christian Wife

Because biblical submission requires the expression of one's gifts on behalf of another, there is great dignity in God's expectations for wives. Seeing this dignity and divine purpose requires examination of the Bible's precise wording about a wife's responsibilities in comparison to the obligations of others.

A Closer Look

A close look at the Bible's words about wives' submission may shock us. In the key passage, "Wives, submit to your husbands" (Eph. 5:22), the word *submit* actually does not appear in the earliest manuscripts of the Bible.[2] The very word we are so ready to debate is not even present. However, the absence of the word does not negate God's purposes. With inspired genius the apostle's word choice underscores the necessity and dignity of a wife's submission.

The word *submit* does appear in the verse preceding the instruction for wives. There the apostle concludes how all Christians can live a Spirit-filled life by saying we should "submit to one another out of reverence for Christ" (Eph. 5:21). Then these words follow: "Wives, to your husbands." There is no question that the apostle intends for wives to apply the submission instruction to their relationship with their husbands. There is also no question that wives are not the only group to whom the submission mandate applies.[3]

The Bible carefully instructs those under others' authority to honor that authority. But God gives equally clear commands about who is to be served by the authority he grants. Husbands must sacrifice their own interests to those under their care, as must parents and masters. To keep the lines of authority clear, no apostle specifically tells husbands to submit to their wives (or parents to submit to children, and so on).[4] However, using the Bible's most powerful analogy, the apostles remind husbands to submit their interests to the good of their wives as Christ sacrificed his prerogatives for the benefit of his people (see Eph. 5:25; 1 Peter 2:21–3:7).

A Common Denominator

Everyone must sacrifice for someone. Wives, children, and servants must submit to husbands, parents, and masters. Husbands, parents, and masters must serve the needs of those for whom they are responsible. Each person must offer whatever gifts, rights, or authority he or she has in service to others for the building up of Christ's kingdom.

The submission responsibilities of a Christian wife do not lessen her value or diminish her dignity. *All* Christians are to submit themselves to the good of others God has placed in their lives. Although the apostle clearly assigns differing purposes to husbands and wives, he just as clearly exempts no one from the Christlike attitudes and actions required of everyone:

> Do nothing out of selfish ambition or vain conceit, but in humility consider others better than yourselves. Each of you should look not only to your own interests, but also to the interests of others.
>
> Your attitude should be the same as that of Christ Jesus: Who, being in very nature God, did not consider equality with God something to be grasped, but made himself nothing, taking the very nature of a servant, being made in human likeness. And being found in appearance as a man, he humbled himself and became obedient to death—even death on a cross!
>
> Philippians 2:3–8

Selfless sacrifice and willing submission to others' best interests is the common denominator of Christian experience, not the reducer of personal worth. This must be our biblical answer to fair-minded concerns of persons such as the businesswoman mentioned at the outset of this chapter. Her concern that the Bible sets up the oppression of women is not foolish, given the way our world equates authority with value. But the world's values are not heaven's, and God does not approve anyone's oppression.

Kathy's thought: Bryan and I have occasionally climbed together up a fourteen-thousand-foot mountain in Colorado. Each time we climbed we were in a group led by a guide. It occurs to me that one way to think of a Christian family is to compare it to such a climb.

Think, perhaps, of the head of the household as the trail guide. The guide assembles and leads the group, following the path marked by a variety of markers along the way: wooden signs, arrows painted on tree trunks, rocks piled by a turn in the path, and, many times, the path itself worn in the ground. As he leads the group up the trail, the guide not only follows the trail markers but also points them out to his charges. He sets the pace of the climb. As the way grows steeper, he encourages his group and cautions them about difficult steps in their path.

The year that Bryan was the guide, he was careful to describe what we would face next along the trail. "Okay," I recall him saying, "we are coming up to the first of three 'stairways.' These are steep, rocky climbs that go straight up this portion of the mountainside. Each stairway is harder than the one before it, but none is very long. We can do this! Just pace yourself and stay with the group. We'll stop to rest at the top of each one. Okay? Let's go!" And so up we went, both forewarned and encouraged by his words.

The guide is responsible to lead the group: following the proper trail, setting the pace, and watching for danger or threatening weather. And similarly the

continues...

The submission the Bible requires of wives gives them obligations as significant as those of any other person. This mutual significance levels rather than stratifies worth. Each person lives for the other. In fact, each must grant greater worth to the interests of the other.

Because each person has a heavenly mandate, all are part of a divine purpose. Each bears the image of God (see Gen. 1:27). Each is purchased at the infinite price of the Son's blood (see Col. 1:20–22). Each is now clothed in Christ's righteousness (see Gal. 3:26–28). Each will receive a heavenly inheritance (see 1 Peter 3:7). Thus, though God does not assign husbands and wives identical responsibilities, Scripture treats both with equal regard (see Eph. 5:33 and 1 Peter 3:7).[5]

The Bible frees men and women from the human grids of power and accomplishment that supposedly determine worth. God removes the comparison and performance price tags we put on ourselves and replaces them with knowledge of our infinite value to God's eternal purposes.

Janette Alexander, wife of the great nineteenth-century theologian Archibald Alexander, was treasured within her family for her scriptural insight. Although she lacked the technical training of her husband, her walk with God gave her special understanding of his Word. When her son also became a famous Bible teacher, he still sought his mother's insights. He said, "Her common sense, in certain matters of this kind, was worth more than all the commentaries in the world."[6]

This wonderful compliment also allows us to see value from God's perspective. Janette Alexander was not the founding professor of a seminary as was her husband. She did not give scholarly training to numerous students. She never had the worldwide reputation for theological insight her husband achieved. Yet she gave him and their children godly care. She helped him acquire the plainness of speech, joy, and compassion that made him so effective as a teacher. And when her son produced commentaries used by preachers to pre-

husband leads—heads—his family: following the trail set out for him in God's Word, teaching the way, encouraging, and watching for the dangers and threats of Satan's temptation and an alluring, sinful world.

And the wife's role? She gets to be the "sweeper"—the hiker who follows, caring for the group, making sure all are keeping up and are well cared for.

As the group climbs, the sweeper makes sure that none are left behind. "We need to slow down a bit," she might tell the guide. "The trail is very rocky here for these young feet." Or, "Look at that view! Let's stop and take a picture; let's slow down and relish the beauty of the view." What a glorious role—to care for the climbers, to point out the beauty of the view, and to enable the guide to guide well!

As a fellow climber up this mountain who is also responsible for those God has given us, I also watch for those trail markers. To take the wrong path could mean hours lost, and in places the trail seems to branch several different directions. Sometimes the way is also quite dangerous as we wind our way up the incline, and a misstep could mean grave injury.

If the guide misses a marker or misreads a sign, it is important for his climbing partner to point to the right way. My husband's role as the head of our household does not mean that I can cease to be diligent in my Christian walk. I should still remain alert for Christ's trail markers, and I must care enough for my husband to alert him if he takes the wrong trail.

pare sermons for countless thousands of people, he sought the wisdom of her heart.

Should we try to determine who did the greater work—Archibald Alexander or Janette Alexander—the arguments would be endless. From heaven's perspective, both persons fulfilled a special purpose whose eternal consequences the human mind cannot begin to compare nor account. Husband and wife submitted to the good of the other and to the design of God. As a result, he granted great usefulness to each in his eternal scheme.

We could multiply the examples of the folly of trying to compare the value of God's varying designs for our lives. For instance, consider which of these persons is more important: Billy Graham or the mother who raised him, the president of a seminary or the elderly woman who prays for him, the choir that sings or the organist that accompanies, the husband who leads or the wife who supports him. The ways our lives are interwoven should teach us that the one who enables service to God is as important as the one who serves.

When Ann Judson accompanied her husband, Adoniram, to India, she could not have predicted her importance in reaching millions with the gospel—nor could she have anticipated the degree of submission her usefulness would require. When tensions arose between England and India, missionaries were often imprisoned.

Adoniram was thrown in a cell so crowded that some prisoners had to stand while others slept. They were deprived of sanitation and water. The oppressive heat made the stench sickening. Captors inflicted further punishment by hanging prisoners, including Adoniram, from their thumbs until the pain broke many of the will to live.

Adoniram survived on words from his wife. Descending into the squalor of the prison and enduring the jeers of the guards, Ann visited her husband when fear made others abandon their spouses. With her eyes she poured love through the prison bars and refreshed his soul with these words. "Do not give up, Adoniram. God will give us the victory." When hope died in others, those oft-repeated words kept Adoniram alive.

Then the visits stopped. For days and then months Ann failed to appear. As anticipation of her visits once kept him alive, now concern for her drove Adoniram to survive each day. When government changes led to his release, he began a desperate search for Ann.

Adoniram soon learned that Ann was dying. As he approached her government-assigned tent, Adoniram met a child so filthy that he did not at first recognize her as his daughter. Inside the tent the conditions were no better. Her body shrunken by disease and malnutrition, Ann lay without movement on tattered blankets. The illness had taken her hair and warped her features so that she was barely recognizable. But Adoniram knew the eyes that still poured out love, and one last time she said the words of support that had sustained him: "Do not give up, Adoniram. God will give us the victory."

Adoniram Judson took his dying wife's words of encouragement as a charge from God. The millions who learned of Jesus as a result of the Judsons' ministry are the spiritual children of Ann Judson. As she lived and died supporting her husband, Ann Judson fulfilled a divine purpose of eternal value.

In Christ's kingdom submission does not lessen the standing of believers; it confirms their significance. Submission will not call every person to the mission field, but it gives every life a mission. Through the sacrifice of personal interests, we fulfill God's purposes for our lives and thus confirm our role in God's plan. Christians' responsibilities vary, but their value does not. As Paul says, "The eye cannot say to the hand, 'I don't need you!'" (1 Cor. 12:21). A wife who supports her husband through a crisis at work, teaches her children to honor his authority, or yields to his decision during a family impasse concedes no inferior status. Instead, she affirms God's call on her life and rightly presumes that her role is as vital for God's results as that of the husband she aids.

Being equal in worth does not require our being the same in function. To conclude otherwise would require us to reason that Christ became inferior when he submitted himself to the Father, or that the Spirit deserves less glory because he submits to the purposes of the Son. Such reasoning is, of course, heretical. The persons of the Trinity are equally divine despite their distinctly different functions.[7] By his trinitarian nature our God has made it abundantly clear that equal value does not require identical roles.[8]

The Glory of a Christian Wife

The dignity of a Christian wife shows not only in the sacrificial calling she shares with all God's people but also in the glory of purpose God grants her. To understand this dignity of purpose, consider the goals our society often advocates for women. In contrast to the biblical perspective that a woman fulfills heavenly purpose in marriage, the modern perspective taken to extremes shackles women's worth to mere standards of income, title, and accomplishment. This perspective teaches women that if they have not sufficiently risen in corporate stature or professional recognition, then they are less valuable than those who have achieved more. Worth becomes directly tied to a row of figures in a bankbook or a line of ink in a year-end report.

While the Bible offers no support for denying women equal opportunity in the workplace,[9] God clearly wants women (and men) to gauge their significance by measures of greater consequence than material possessions or a societal pecking order (see Matt. 16:26; 1 Tim. 6:17–19). When personal worth gets linked to personal success, then one's dignity exists simply in comparisons to others. And, as a consequence, our value rests on transient personal and economic factors beyond anyone's control. In contrast, God wants us to base our dignity on his eternal regard.

A subtle yet spiritually debilitating change occurs in a woman when her dignity is measured by wealth, number of children, size of house, personal accomplishments, or a husband's prestige. Such measurements turn a woman's attention from God's purposes to her own.

The indignity of this self-focus can become apparent in as unlikely a source as an avant-garde woman's magazine. A book reviewer in just such a magazine noted that early feminist books had been about women gaining access to power and opportunity. But in assessing newer books, she concluded:

> Feminism is no longer a battle for equal opportunity in a male-dominated society, but a kind of 12-step recovery program for wounded women. . . . "There is an endless appetite for self-help books. . . ." They do not offer women still struggling in an unfair world any clarion call to arms. Instead they urge women to redefine their inner lives.[10]

This review was written by an advocate of modern feminism. How sad (and revealing) that, at least in this reviewer's estimation, a cause that began with altruistic concern for universal equality now is but another journey into me-ism.[11] Whether feminist efforts return to seeking justice for all or stay focused on inner healing cannot be predicted. What is plain to everyone is the indignity of pouring one's life and demands into the vain, cloying pursuit of "what's in it for me."

Gary and Betsy Ricucci comment further on the consequences of defining a woman's (or man's) significance only by personal gain:

> Contrary to popular opinion, woman was not created for her own fulfillment. (That goes for the men, too!) She was created to be a helper and a nurturer. Now that is not an easy assignment to accept. We tend to bristle and think, There must be something more significant than that! What homemaker hasn't found herself asking, after the fiftieth load of laundry in a week or when facing yet another sink full of dirty dishes, "Is there anything significant about what I'm doing here?" Yet in God's eyes, nothing is more significant than servanthood. The path to genuine greatness lies in serving.
>
> Grasping for power or recognition is natural. Servanthood is supernatural. So many women are missing out on the supernatural today because they are caught up in the "search for significance." Ironically, the more they search for it, the less satisfied they feel. Why? Significance is found in giving your life away, not in selfishly trying to find personal happiness.[12]

Whether man or woman, no one is more disrespected than an individual driven by selfishness. We sense this truth in the comic-book life of a Donald Trump, who gains power and wealth at the expense of our respect; we see the opposite in the life of a Mother Teresa, who received the honor of the world though she had nothing. Such examples enable us to understand the dignity God grants to the wife who submits herself to the good of her husband and family. The Bible says they will rise up and call her blessed (see Prov. 31:28). Her dignity is assured in the blessing of the ones to whom she gives herself. Her glory resides in her unwillingness to be driven by any priorities other than God's. Heaven is reflected in her focus on others.

The Church's Affirmation

Affirmation of the glory of a wife who lives for another should be one of the great ministries of the church. Sadly, we have trouble offering it. Some branches of the church seem so caught up in fighting for women's rights that they sound little different from the secular voices that make self-fulfillment life's highest aim. Other branches of the church are so threatened by women's movements that their chief concern seems to be keeping women "in their place." As a consequence, churches can become much more focused on attacking capable women than at discerning how their gifts may be biblically employed for Christ's purposes.

Because we have trouble remembering that submission is an arranging of one's gifts under the purposes of God rather than a universal code of behaviors, we create tensions that needlessly deny women opportunities to serve God. We damage our own wives and daughters as a result. My wife says to me, "Bryan, it doesn't matter what I do; there are people in our church who will accuse me of not fulfilling my proper role. If I devote myself entirely to family care, some women in the church will say I have abandoned my potential in the workplace and am contributing to the subjugation of my own daughters. If I work outside the home—even part-time—others will accuse me of forsaking Scripture and giving in to cultural pressures. For women in the church today, all choices are attackable."

In the face of such conflict and confusion, the church must speak clearly of the nobility of a life lived for the good of another. Jesus said anyone who follows him must "deny himself" (Matt. 16:24; Mark 8:34; Luke 9:23). More than a call to an occasional act of charity, this is a charge to put God's priorities above our own on a daily basis. We live according to God's design with the faith that there is nothing more important that we can do. This means my own calling is to assure my wife that there is nothing more valuable to our family than her fulfilling her biblical responsibilities in our home.

> **Kathy's thought:** The attacks on our choices can be very subtle. As I have been asked to fill out forms—school forms, insurance forms at the doctor's office, credit card applications at the local Sam's Club— the lines go something like this: Name, Address, Home phone, Employer, Employer's address, Employer's phone number, and so on. At times during our lives I have had an employer to record, but at other times I have been a full-time, stay-at-home mom and homemaker, and during those times my forms have blank lines.
>
> There is something about those blank lines that seems almost accusatory, as though I have admitted to having a void in my life, or am doing nothing important. (I have been known to fill in those blanks as follows: Employer: the Lord, Employer's address: heaven, Employer's phone: John 3:16.) I believe wholeheartedly that there are times when it is best to be a full-time, stay-at-home wife and mother, and yet . . . there are those blank lines. My challenge is to not allow a paper form to dictate what is best biblically for my family—or for me.

The Husband's Affirmation

A Christian woman said to me recently, "I understand why so many women struggle with what the Bible says about submission, but I have never struggled with submitting to my husband because he lets me know how much he respects me." That husband lives as Scripture requires.

The apostle Peter says, "Husbands, . . . be considerate as you live with your wives, and treat them with respect" (1 Peter 3:7). These words require me to tell my wife how much I respect her sacrifices for the good of our family. I need to remember that it caused consternation among her college instructors when she did not pursue a concert career that would have conflicted with our church ministry. I should relish the creative ways that she has used her musical gifts to bring glory to God and good to our family. When my early jobs offered meager financial support to our family, she taught music lessons for extra income. For many years she has led children and adult choirs, often without pay, to enable our children and our church to glorify God. She has performed countless solos, hymn accompaniments, Christmas programs, and Easter cantatas for the pure joy of sharing her music with others. She has even let me croak Broadway tunes with her at our home piano. All this she has done while raising four children to love the Lord—the greatest instruments of her praise.

Depending on the ages of our children, our financial needs, and the demands of my job, Kathy has varied the allocation of her time and energies to occupations outside our home. Yet she has never wavered in submitting her own interests to the needs of those God has entrusted to her care. In a confusing age others may question her choices, but I respect them—and her. I pray that she will never doubt the glorious regard that I have for her because heaven itself honors her support of her husband and home.

Heaven's Honor

The Puritan preacher John Angell James sought to summarize the glory of a wife who lives according to God's priorities:

Man is neither safe in himself, nor profitable to others, when he lives dissociated from that benign influence which is to be found in woman's presence and character. . . . But it is not woman . . . separated from those divine teachings which make all hearts wise, that can lay claim to the exercise of such influence. But when she adds to the traits of sympathy, forbearance, and warm affection, which characterize her, the strength and wisdom of a well-cultivated intellect, and the still higher attributes of religious faith and holy love, it is not easy to limit the good she may do in all situations, and in all periods of life.[13]

Historically, when Scripture has been rightly interpreted and the church has been rightly motivated, women have been granted honor. Present-day Christians must take care that cultural forces do not press us away from this biblical perspective. Even in churches holding dear the Scriptures that speak of the preciousness of women in God's family

Kathy's thought: It has been good for me through the years to reflect on the words of Ecclesiastes: "There is a time for everything, and a season for every activity under heaven" (3:1). There are seasons of life, and life is not the same from one season to another. And every activity, according to the writer of Ecclesiastes, does *not* have to be done during one season. There are, I think, multiple layers of truth in that one verse.

Women older than I used to say to me, "Enjoy your children while they are little, because they grow up so fast!" At the time, I had several little children, and I didn't fully appreciate their meaning. Life was too hectic for me even to have the time to imagine a life with grown-up children, although the mere concept sounded rather restful. I needed to turn down many opportunities to serve, whether in Bible studies, music performances, or lunches with friends. All these commitments were good things, but I was not comfortable with what they would mean to our family.

When our children reached elementary and middle school, they needed less of my time, and it became more reasonable for me to do more

continues...

economy, women report they experience degrading jests and insensitivity. We may understand (but cannot accept) the explanation that Bible-believing churches are overreacting to the feminist pressures of our society. We cannot uphold biblical priorities by embarrassing, intimidating, and demoralizing anyone God places among us. Such actions reveal our insecurity more than they promote orthodoxy. We cannot expect Christian wives to treasure the duties God has designed for them if the church does not defend the dignity of women's responsibilities and give honor to those who assume them.

outside our home. I served for ten years as music director at our church, and it was a blessed and fulfilling time for us.

When I needed to be at home again with older teens and children preparing for college, I left the music job, and it was the right decision for that season. The Lord has given me great peace and assurance with these decisions. He has reminded me that my husband and our children—five precious souls on their way to eternity—are precious to him, and that I serve my God by loving and caring for them. I don't know what the seasons ahead will bring or what he will ask me to do, but I am very content to wait on him and his timing.

In the summer of 1996, our friend Joan Hollinshead took her husband, Tom, for a walk in a nearby park. Seriously disabled by a stroke at an age that was decades before such catastrophes usually strike, Tom was grateful for the support of his wife that enabled the outing after months of rehabilitation. To add to their fun, Joan also took along the dog that delighted Tom. The three slowly ambled down the mile-long walking path circling the park, but the challenge was still greater than they anticipated.

Halfway around the park Tom's legs began to tremble. His strength evaporated and he could go no farther. He now needed Joan's help more than ever. Joan knew Tom needed medical attention quickly but she had no way to get him back to their car. Supporting him even a short distance to a place where he could sit had proved awkward with the now-anxious dog dancing around their feet. Not having alternatives, Joan prepared to leave Tom to go get help. In desperation, she sought the Lord's help for both of them with a quickly voiced prayer. "Dear Lord," she said, "I don't know what to do. Please send your angels to help us."

When she lifted her head from prayer, a policeman on a motorcycle was coming down the path. The officer quickly summoned help and the emergency passed.

Then Joan asked the policeman, "What made you come down this walking path on your motorcycle? I have never seen a policeman in this part of the park."

The officer replied, "We have wanted a greater police presence in the park, so the city council just authorized us to patrol these paths. My ride tonight was our very first patrol."

Joan thought, *Mr. Policeman, you may have thought the authorization came from the city council, but I think it came from a higher authority.*

That day heaven dramatically honored the many kinds of physical and spiritual support a Christian wife gave her husband. What I wish for her and for every wife who gives herself for the good of her spouse — in a thousand less dramatic ways — is the knowledge that heaven honors each gift. God reflects his own glory in the wife who lives for another.

6

A WOMAN'S DESIRE

The Honor of Another

AN OLD COMMERCIAL for car wax depicts a young woman preparing to sell her car. Aged and dull, the vehicle that she has used for years holds no more allure for her. Yet when she uses the "miracle" wax to put shine back on the finish, the new gloss revives her affection. She throws away the "For Sale" sign and drives away, happy with her car.

The commercial rings true about the way our hearts function. We love what we invest in. When we give ourselves for the satisfaction, security, and development of other persons, we do more than build their self-esteem; we add to our esteem of them. By contributing to another's sense of worth, we also delight in that person more. Applied to marriage, these truths become the threads that knit and repair our relationships.

When a woman supports and affirms her spouse, her love for him deepens. The regard she gives not only expresses her love but builds it. When she withholds regard, love diminishes. For this reason, the Bible instructs wives to search for the affection that strengthens marriage, not in the deserving of her husband but in the desires of her heart (see 1 Peter 3:1–6). This instruction resonates with the deeper truth that a wife longs to respect her husband because intuitively she knows her capacity to love depends on that regard. The Bible's command for respect harmonizes with what an unselfish and unwounded heart wants.

To Respect Her Husband

As the apostle Paul concludes comments on marriage in the book of Ephesians, he reminds men to "love" their wives, but he tells women to "respect" their husbands (5:33). He seems to deal with each gender at its weak points. A man's temptation is to use the power of his position and physique to enforce dictatorial rule or to indulge passive self-absorption. A woman's temptation is often to use the power of words and emotions to shame her husband into doing as she wishes. Paul allows neither "power play" by commanding men to love and women to respect their spouses.

The power of the forces the apostle seeks to curb were dramatically evident to Kathy and me early in our marriage. Our small salaries required us to live in a cheap apartment in a poor part of town. There the paper-thin walls of the housing complex gave us an ear-opening perspective on others' lives. Our sheltered suburban backgrounds did not prepare us for the vileness and violence the families around us considered normal.

Most disconcerting was the minister's family that lived below us. Most of the fights between that husband and wife were about who was the better witness. We usually tried to ignore the shouts and slaps until we would hear him choking her. Then we would try to find some way to intervene. We dropped books on the floor, called on the phone, or borrowed cups of sugar at very odd times. Occasionally we called the police.

The experience sickened us but it also matured us. As we listened to the husband and wife shout their way to the brutal climax of what became almost nightly conflicts, we began to recognize a pattern. The husband would get irritated with something his wife or children had done. He would shout his disapproval. The wife in turn would begin to criticize him with equal volume and at greater length. Her readiness to escalate the verbal combat surprised Kathy and me. We would sometimes turn to one another and say, "Why does she taunt him so? She knows he is going to hit her."

We did not know what we have since learned about abusive homes: as a man will try to dominate a woman with strength, a woman will try to control a man with shame. The verbal criticism our downstairs neighbor directed at her husband was her weapon to make her husband back down. Sometimes it worked—sometimes it did not.

Even if violence is not present (though too often it is), the ways these spouses tried to control each other are reflected in many marriages. Men exert power with intimidation or intransigence. (For counsel on dealing with abuse, see the end of this chapter.) Women use a demeaning look, a cutting

Kathy's thought: I think there is an even more self-serving aspect to shaming one's mate. I have often comforted a child saddened by a cruel remark from a playmate by pointing out that a person sometimes makes fun of another in order to feel better about himself. A wife who belittles her husband may, even without knowing it, be seeking to feel better about herself in comparison. "See how I am smarter (or wittier or more capable) than he," she implies. Her own poor self-image is desperate for affirmation, even if she seems to gain it by demeaning the very one who could provide her support. She takes control of her self-image by proving to herself that she is superior to her mate.

remark, an accusation, or an embarrassing reminder to diminish a man so he becomes less sure of himself and more controllable.

Sadly, these factors often become cyclical. Insecure men react to their sense of being diminished by becoming more dominating. This in turn gives a wife more opportunity to needle and shame, which subsequently triggers more abuse. When this cycle is in effect to any degree, the marriage becomes a daily tug-of-war for power. Power may be expressed through intimidation or manipulation. Control measures may take the form of screaming or scheming, silence or secrecy, whining or withdrawal, violence or victimization. Whether the means are active or passive, the goal of each of these behaviors remains the same—controlling the other person.

For His Sake

Against all of these control mechanisms, the Bible crusades for a different ruling force: love (see Eph. 5:1–2). Scripture does not allow a Christian husband to intimidate or ignore his wife to serve his own interests. The Bible does not give a Christian wife approval to diminish or shame her husband to get her way. God commands selfless care that excludes striving for spousal control.

Early in our marriage my wife and I agreed not to belittle one another in public even in jest. Our agreement came after noticing how often in group settings our friends used ridicule (often disguised as teasing) to get an edge over one another. Remarks about appearance, reminders of a past embarrassment, or drawing attention to a dumb comment are standard ways that couples use the shield of social conversation to jab at each other's faults and foibles. My wife and I actually enjoy teasing one another, but we do not kid in a way that is demeaning for the sake of a laugh from others.

I have to be honest with my wife and say simply that I need her respect. Women may not recognize how much husbands are affected by their wives' respect—or lack of it. There have been moments in my life when I felt the only things of value I had left were the respect and love of my wife. When a church's leadership was convinced I was wrong, when I felt I had sacrificed my career for a cause everyone else thought was foolish, when others made me doubt my own competence, when I delivered awful sermons, when I was guilty of sin that exposed the weakness of my faith—in each of those moments the respect of my wife has meant everything. She has loved me enough to look past my weaknesses, stupidities, and failures to see traits in me that she could still respect. Not only has her consistent respect secured our love; it has also given me confidence and strength. I could neither do nor be what God required were it not for my wife's faithful regard for me.

Husbands are enabled by the respect of their wives. This is why God commands

Kathy's thought: I need to push the pause button here. I have read this section many, many times; Bryan has conveyed this sentiment directly to me and in various talks and panel discussions. I never know how to express (without tears) my response to this thought—that I have somehow made him stronger; that I have made him able to be and do what God requires of him. My husband is the finest, most splendid man I know, and that the Lord of the universe would use me to enable my husband to serve him is so overwhelming.

We recently heard a beautiful young bride and groom promise in their vows to be a "vessel of God's grace" to one another. One day I will come up with the words to express adequately what this phrase means to me; then *I* will write a book too and call it *A Happy Vessel in the Hands of Her Maker*.

Kathy's thought: I recently attended a seminar involving women of different ages and stages of life. The discussion turned to things the Lord has taught us in our walk with him. Several women talked about learning the importance of respecting their husbands. One dear friend put it this way: "I wish I had learned sooner how much my husband desires and needs my respect. I thought he was just out doing his thing, and that he was getting the respect and affirmation he needed from his job, his boss, and his friends. But what he really needed and wanted was *my* respect, *my* affirmation, *my* support. I know that now, and he's a much happier man. We're a happier couple."

wives to give their husbands such regard. Men were made in need of a helper to fulfill God's purposes (see Gen. 2:18). A wife who understands this can rejoice that her respect is vital for the man she loves to honor God well. A wife who does not understand that God designed husbands to thrive through her respect too often discovers that her husband will find other sources for the respect he requires.

Hollywood stereotypes to the contrary, my counseling experience indicates married men typically do not get involved in extramarital relationships with women more beautiful and sophisticated than their wives. Men have affairs with women who make them feel important and competent—in a word, respected. Men in such affairs will acknowledge they are involved with someone who does not "measure up" to their wives in beauty, intelligence, or social standing. Still, the man's need for respect from a woman drives him to one who knows him less well but treats him more highly than his wife.

A man's need never excuses his betrayal, nor does his guilt prove his wife's neglect. But the woman who loves her husband and wants to guard their marriage from sin strives to make her regard his lifeline to self-respect. Staying interested in a husband's career, rejoicing in his successes, cheerleading his ambitions, listening to his dreams, honoring his decisions, admiring his physical appearance, and making a joyous offering of love by overlooking flaws in each of these areas are powerful seductions available to every wife.

For Her Sake

I do not want to give the impression that a wife should give her husband respect merely to serve his ego. Of greater consideration to Scripture is the effect giving respect has on a wife's own heart. Susan Hunt offers this poignant account by an unnamed writer:

> Before marriage I was attracted to my husband's strong personality. After marriage this same personality overwhelmed me. I began believing the lie that Eve believed in the Garden—I could not be fulfilled doing it God's way. I believed the lies that I would have to fight for my rights and that it was my responsibility to destroy my husband's ego, so I did everything I could to belittle him. I corrected him in public. I rarely expressed admiration or appreciation. In trying to destroy his pride, I was destroying his manhood and elevating my own pride. I convinced myself that when he changed, I would be a great wife. I was less and less interested in him. There were no feelings of affection or love. I would rather have gone to an execution than to bed with my husband. I turned off all the music and wore flannel nightgowns. I resented the fact that my husband was so needy, ignoring the truth that perfect Adam also had needs.[1]

The husband is not the only one who benefits from the respect of a godly wife; she benefits too. The respect a wife offers her husband is vital for finding the deeper levels of marital bliss for which her heart yearns. The more she treasures her husband, the more precious and fulfilling a woman will find their union. The woman who longs for deep satisfaction in her marriage must provide the support that secures the relationship for which she longs. Conversely the woman who does not offer her husband respect denies herself the marital intimacy she desires.

These principles apply to men as well as women. A man who does not consider his wife worthy of his honor will also lose his desire for intimacy with her. God requires each marriage partner to respect the other. The apostle Peter writes, "Husbands, in the same way be considerate as you live with your wives, and treat them with respect as the weaker partner and as heirs with you of the gracious gift of life, so that nothing will hinder your prayers" (1 Peter 3:7).

The obligations of mutual regard are not less for either spouse, but these obligations do vary. Peter's words remind us that each husband should respect his wife: 1) for the tenderness and sensitivity she brings to their home; 2) for the support she offers that gives her a right to inherit the same spiritual blessings as he; and 3) for the opportunity his care of her provides for him to cultivate his own spiritual relationship with the Lord.

Love and honor are inextricably linked. The women the Bible presents as most desirable are those most respected by their husbands (see Prov. 31:10–31; Song of Sol. 7:1–9). Men are attracted to those they honor and are repulsed by those they disrespect. Physical attraction, though powerful, will not maintain a relationship in which mutual respect has died. For this reason, women the Bible most honors for their love also have the highest respect for their spouses (1 Peter 3:5–6).

As I write these words, the marriages of some of my friends are coming unglued. At almost any time in my adult life I could say this. The causes are too numerous to count, but consistent in almost all of these sad scenarios are years of battle for control of the home. The couples presently struggling are successful and blessed with beautiful children. All the spouses consider themselves committed Christians. Yet despite these wonderful gifts, these couples' homes have become battlegrounds for power, with each personal gift and talent a weapon in the war.

Financial success and credit accounts allow each of these spouses to be independent and self-indulgent. Children's activities have become excuses for parents to ignore each other, or children's antics become reasons to blame each other. Because they are intelligent and articulate, the couples are able to use arguments, excuses, and jests to back each other into embarrassing corners. Each spouse uses the faith commitment of the other like a flashlight to expose inconsistencies or to reveal guilt that will leverage some concession. Mutual respect is miles away, buried under layers of bitterness neither spouse will disturb lest he or she lose ground in the battle for control.

These people will all stand before the Lord one day to give an account of their role in these domestic battles. Husbands will need to explain why their leadership turned self-serving or severe. Wives must answer whether they ceased to honor because they wanted control more than love.

All Christian women must remember that the corrupted values of our world tempt each heart to desire control. After Adam and Eve sinned, God said that from then on women would desire their husbands' position and authority.[2] God's redeeming influence restores in a woman an appreciation for the headship God designed for her husband, and it gives the husband a heart for servant leadership. This means peace will not come to any marriage until each partner seeks to serve rather than to sway the other. The service that brings a wife fulfillment begins with recognition that the love for which her heart longs cannot flourish without the respect for her husband that God requires.

Every day I try to tell my wife that I love her. I know that she delights to hear it, though, candidly, I do not have the same depth of appreciation for these words that she does. My expression of love for her touches something deep in her heart that I (as a sometimes less-than-sensitive man) do not fully comprehend. I say the words because I love bringing her joy, not because I entirely understand how or why they transmit that joy.

In a similar way I wish that women understood that a man's confidence of his wife's respect is the ground on which he plants his feet to meet life's challenges. As a husband's assurances of his love provide a wife security and comfort for her trials, her respect is his fortress. The firmer the ground of his wife's respect, the more able the husband is to react with proper strength or tenderness to his challenges. The respect a wife shows her husband secures her marriage in ways more powerful than most women (or men) fully comprehend.

The apostle Paul spoke with great understanding of men and women when he concluded, "Each [man] . . . must love his wife as he loves himself, and the wife must respect her husband" (Eph. 5:33). The words remind husbands and wives to express care for one another in the ways that touch each other's heart most deeply. When a woman senses that her marriage has yet to know its full riches—or when her relationship with her husband has grown cold—God offers this powerful help: wives, respect your husbands.

To Reverence Her Husband

God reveals the importance of a woman's regard for her husband in one startling word. The word translated "respect" actually comes from the same term the apostle Paul used a few sentences earlier to say we must "reverence" Christ (Eph. 5:21). Reverence requires holy awe.

The apostle's language causes me to remember a woman in our church who was seeking to divorce her husband without biblical cause. When church leaders urged her to love her husband, she replied, "Love him?! I can't even stomach him. Just the thought of him makes me ill." I can only imagine how much stronger her reaction would have been if we had urged her to reverence him!

We can easily make sense of the word *reverence* when it refers to Christ. We understand how and why we are to honor our Savior. But why would Paul say a wife should *reverence* her husband when no man is worthy of such regard?

The Reasons for Reverence

Surely one reason Paul urges reverence is that he wants to emphasize the regard due biblical headship. The Bible identifies headship as a holy office in the home, and no one should slight what the Bible says we should revere. The wife has holy obligations in terms of both her attitudes and her actions toward her husband.

Another possible reason the apostle uses the word *reverence* is to underscore that the spiritual head of the home must give account to God for the spiritual nurture of his family. The wife who has the vision to perceive this will understand why her husband should be revered. We might compare her reverence to that of a young Olympian's parents who are awestruck by the achievements of their own child who performs before millions under the scrutiny of human judges. So a wife, who sees with spiritual eyes, can perceive the breathtaking glory of her husband's performance of his spiritual duties before both the hosts of heaven and the Judge of the universe. Every husband is accountable to God for the spiritual guidance he gives his family. The holiness and gravity of his obligations are so awesome that they require honor, even though he carries them out imperfectly.

The Resources for Reverence

The husband's certain imperfections provide the best reason for the Bible's use of *reverence* to describe how a wife should regard her husband. The term points a wife back to the source of her esteem for her husband—and reminds her the source is *not* him or his worthiness.

The word *reverence* at the conclusion of the apostle's discussion of marriage echoes his introduction. There Paul encourages believers to "submit to one another out of reverence for Christ" (Eph. 5:21). By repeating this theme in the final instruction to wives, the apostle says, in effect, "The reverence you have for your husband should find its source not in who he is, in what he does, or in how deserving he is. Reverence is rooted in your relationship with the Savior. The honor you show your husband ultimately comes from your desire to please God."

Rooting a wife's regard for her husband in her relationship with the Savior answers a question I recognize some readers have had since the opening of this chapter: what should I do if my husband is undeserving of my respect, much less my reverence? For some the question arises from deep pain. For others the question comes from an honest evaluation of a husband's character. For still others the question stems from an unwillingness to be bound by God's Word. Whether the question comes from good motives or ill, the answer remains the same. God requires a wife to honor her husband, not because of the goodness he possesses but because of the grace he needs.

Though many men are worthy of their wives' respect, none are worthy of their wives' reverence. God's command to give such undeserved regard requires us to recognize that the honor is an unmerited gift rather than an earned deference. Gary Thomas writes,

> I reach out to others because God has loved me and has asked me to love others in return, not because the people I am loving are "worthy" of love. . . . God is always worthy of being obeyed and served, so when I act out of obedience to him, the person who receives my service doesn't have to be deserving—they're benefiting from what I owe God. Yes, this truth is hard to apply in marriage, where demands and expectations are so plentiful, but I try to remind myself of this fact: God is always worthy of being obeyed, and God calls me to serve my spouse—so regardless of how she treats me at any particular moment, I am called to respond as a servant.
>
> Jesus' example has challenged me greatly in this regard. None of the disciples deserved to have their feet washed at the Last Supper—all of them would abandon him within a few hours. . . . In fact, Jesus even washed the feet of Judas, who was just hours away from betraying him. . . . If you are in a one-sided marriage where you feel you're giving and never

receiving, my heart goes out to you. You can partially redeem such a situation by becoming more God-oriented. . . . If the heart of Christianity is service, any situation that shapes the spirit of a servant is worthwhile—even a lopsided marriage.[3]

Just as a husband's qualities cannot kindle his wife's reverence, neither should his faults quench it. This does not mean that a wife should approve of her husband's errors or participate in his ungodliness. She should, however, recognize that in her service to the Savior, she is a conduit of his grace to her spouse as long as God binds her to him. A husband experiences God's unmerited favor through the undeserved honor a wife gives him. Respecting the characteristics of a spouse that are honorable, forgiving the flaws that cannot be honored, and caring for the man regardless of his dishonor—these bless the man, but in greater measure they reverence God (see 1 Peter 3:9).

The most quoted line from the classic movie *Chariots of Fire* was Eric Liddell's explanation of why he ran: "Because when I run, I feel God's pleasure." Those words echoed in my mind when I accompanied a distraught husband to his home to confess his failures to his wife. He had lost his job, spent his last dollar on diversions to make him forget, and returned home expecting his wife to add her scorn to the weight of his self-defeat. Instead, she told him that she loved him.

Kathy's thought: I think I might also point to Matthew 25, when the righteous ask, "Lord, when did we see you hungry and feed you, or thirsty and give you something to drink? When did we see you a stranger and invite you in, or needing clothes and clothe you?" (vv. 37–38). The King will reply, "I tell you the truth, whatever you did for one of the least of these brothers of mine, you did for me" (v. 40).

Why is it easy to apply these verses to our hearts when we think of sending money to orphanages in Africa, and yet we forget—or resist believing—that honoring our husbands is honoring God? Why should I struggle to love him when he is unlovable, if loving him is what Christ has asked me to do? Why is it hard to forgive him, when Christ has forgiven me? How can I not reverence my husband—the man God gave me—when Scripture tells me that by reverencing him, I am serving and obeying and reverencing my Lord?

He collapsed sobbing into a chair. Then, as I looked on, she placed a hand on his shoulder and for the next half hour reminded him of the good she loved in him.

The words the wife spoke did as much to strengthen her heart as they did to rebuild the young man's self-respect. She told him how she admired his sensitivity and care for their children. She reminded him of the ways he made her laugh and of moments their family treasured. She listed the people who believed in him. Simply by recounting what she did respect in this terribly flawed man, the wife's eyes glistened with renewed love. He knew that he was undeserving of this kind of love. At one point he objected to her words by saying, "I don't want you to love me so much." She responded simply, "God does." She gave her husband respect not only because he needed it but because she knew God delighted in her doing so.

This divine-source motivation permeates all of the apostle Paul's thought and takes priority over all other reasons for honoring one another. His startling command for wives to hold their husbands in "holy awe" is the bloom of thoughts planted earlier. He writes, "Be imitators of God, therefore, as dearly loved children and live a life of love, just as Christ loved us and gave himself up for us as a fragrant offering and sacrifice to God" (Eph. 5:1–2). The joy we take from the Lord's love is the strength and motive for our own. Wives reverence their husbands (and husbands give themselves for their wives) out of reverence for what Christ has done for us. Ultimately all of us are to be communicating Christ's sacrificial work to each other out of love for him. Just as Jesus' sacrifice was a pleasing fragrance to God, so sacrificial care brings pleasure to the God of grace. And the knowledge of his pleasure in us provides the joy that is our strength for his purposes.

I sensed some of this divine pleasure at a Valentine's social my wife and I attended. Those present at the banquet took much delight in listening to an older couple sing their own version of "Do You Love Me?" from the musical *Fiddler on the Roof*. At the point of the song where the stage characters are supposed to sing, "After twenty-five years it's nice to know [that you love me]," this couple substituted their own marriage's stats and sang, "After forty-eight years it's nice to know." In a church dominated by young marriages that have not yet stood the test of years, the enduring love of this couple was more than endearing. It was inspiring. When they hit the last notes of the song, the room exploded in a standing ovation as we cheered for a love that had so powerfully encouraged us and had so radiantly persevered in them.

We were about to discover there was more for them to endure. Just a few minutes later their forty-one-year-old son also went on the stage to tell us about his current battle with cancer and the hope that he still claimed as a result of his parents' life of faith. After the social, I spoke to the parents privately in a remote hallway of the church where we were gathering our coats. I told the couple that I had been surprised by their son's cancer report. They said that the news was only days old to them as well. There had been no history or warning signs to prepare them—just an out-of-the-blue telephone call: "Mom and Dad, I have cancer."

As they told me this account of their beloved son, the recentness of the news with its shock, grief, and fear welled in the couple. The man, usually so stoic, could not keep tears from his eyes. When his wife saw his pain and the embarrass-

Dealing with Abuse

Know Your Rights

The Bible does not require a woman to remain in an abusive marriage. Jesus allows divorce on the basis of adultery (see Matt. 5:32), and the apostle Paul also identifies willful and irremediable desertion as a form of marriage-covenant breaking that may serve as grounds (see 1 Cor. 7:15). It is my understanding of these Scriptures that severe emotional and physical abuse are included as forms of desertion of the marriage covenant and provide grounds for separation or dissolution of a marriage (see 1 Cor. 7:10–11).

Know Your Lord

God's allowance for divorce in the face of marital unfaithfulness and desertion (in all their forms) does not require the one who has been sinned against to end a marriage. All Christians are representatives of their Savior. Where Christ's grace is better represented by forgiveness and perseverance, a person sinned against may choose to remain in a difficult marriage for the sake of showing Christ's reconciling love to a sinful spouse—or to children and the watching world. Christ may call us to temporal sacrifice and service for the sake of sharing eternal love.

Know Your Limits

Whether to endure or end a difficult marriage should never be decided alone. Those who are in difficult marriages may be the least ready to determine what they should do. Sin and selfishness can tempt one to label as "abuse" human fault and weakness that are not truly threats to any who, for Christ's sake, are willing to consider the needs of others higher than their own (see Phil. 2:3–4). However, abuse can create a skewed reality in the mind of a victim, causing her (or him) to accept or excuse mistreatment. Selfishness inflates accusations of abuse, but true abuse also robs its victims of perspective and objectivity. No one should try to handle abuse without talking to a pastor, a church officer, a counselor, or other mature believers.

Know Your Resources

If you are in immediate danger, call the police or get out of the situation. Paul teaches that the civil authorities are instruments of God's purpose to restrain evil (see Rom. 13:4). Additionally, the God who sanctifies life requires us to defend our lives and our children. Separation may be needed for an extended time both for safety and to allow effective counseling for all parties. Responsible church authorities should be told of abuse so they can protect victims (and correct abusers) by providing family intervention, counseling, prayer, support, and, if needed, safety and church discipline. The yellow pages and the Internet will also provide numerous confidential social services for families with abuse problems.

Know Your Status

You are not alone. Experts say abuse is present in almost 20 percent of marriages, and this includes many Christian marriages. Both women (85 percent of the time) and men can suffer from domestic violence.[4] Shame, false guilt, and fear are the most common reasons that spouses do not seek help for abuse that damages them, their families, and their abuser. Willingness to confront abuse for the sake of the purposes God intends to promote in our lives and family comes with the confidence that we are eternally loved by God and eternally secure in his care. Refusing to accept abuse in our lives and families is biblical. Jesus will not forsake you because you take steps to confront an abuser and end abuse.

ment of his tears, she touched his arm. It was such a small and subtle gesture, and yet I could almost see the strength flow from her as the man then collected himself and spoke again of their faith in God's care.

The wife, I am sure, wanted to cry as much as (if not more than) her husband. The tears would have been far more typical of her, and she had no less need to be comforted by him. Yet in that moment he needed her strength, and in that reassuring touch she sacrificed the expression of her own grief to minister to his pain. In their oneness she knew just how to help him and how to preserve his respect in the midst of her own hurting. The simple gesture represented a duty of deep love, a dignifying of him that dignified her, and a desire to serve her husband that had been nurtured through a lifetime of serving God.

Who witnessed this wife's giving of herself in that caring touch in the hall? I did, and maybe one or two others, but for her I again heard applause—another standing ovation. This applause known only to the heart was exploding from the portals of heaven as its hosts rejoiced for a wife who in those moments submitted her right to grieve to her husband's need for support. I hope with her spiritual ears she heard it too. On that day I pray that she sensed heaven's regard for the beauty of her service. On this day may you who read these words also know and claim the eternal value, scriptural glory, and personal delight of every wife who submits to her husband out of reverence for the Lord.

SACRIFICIAL PARTNERS

Shared Love

Submit to one another out of reverence for Christ.

Ephesians 5:21

I N   H E R   B O O K *The True Woman,* Susan Hunt tells of our mutual friend Rosalie Cassels.[1] For more than eighty years Rosalie was a member of the Rosehill Presbyterian Church in Columbia, South Carolina. Her father began the church as a Sunday school class for poor children.

In her early adult years, Rosalie devoted herself to the spiritual training of women. She became a leader of women's organizations in her denomination. Because of her husband's success in business, she was also able to travel repeatedly to the mission field on behalf of women. But her care was not limited to those like her in near or distant lands. From 1947 to 1967 Rosalie served as the director of the International Christian Conference for Negro Women at Benedict College. This summer institute trained hundreds for Christian service.

Rosalie's passion for interracial ministry was sparked by the experience of trying to find help for a maid she loved. One day the maid became ill, and Rosalie drove her to see the town doctor. Along the way the illness of the maid required her to seek a restroom. Again and again Rosalie stopped to ask assistance, but none of the Caucasian-owned businesses would allow the needy black woman to use their facilities. From that point on Rosalie knew her mission for Christ was as close as her own community.

Rosalie worked for racial justice in the Deep South before and through the civil rights movement because she believed the gospel should know no social barriers. For her efforts Rosalie was often ostracized by area Christians. Disdainful murmurs often rose when she entered a restaurant.

As Rosalie aged, her activities necessarily curtailed, but not her zeal for God's work. She taught a Sunday school class in her church for forty years and, when she was no longer able to do that, still found ways to share her knowledge. She spent every Saturday with her housekeeper, Bennie. With Rosalie's books spread about them, the two women would sit together in Rosalie's home preparing for the class Bennie would teach in her church the next day. Forty years' worth of lesson plans and Bible study helps were selflessly, extravagantly shared with Bennie. The knowledge and commitments of a lifetime still ripple through many lives because of the love of Rosalie for the Lord and his people.

Rosalie Cassels's life epitomizes for me what the third portion of this book addresses. When partnerships reflect the priorities of Christ, they have an impact on many other lives. Rosalie's parents committed themselves to the care of the poor in the establishment of a church. That church then taught others—including their daughter—to share the love of Jesus. When Rosalie took that love into a marriage with a man who was also committed to her and the Lord's work, the love of Christ spread farther and reverberates still.

Through Rosalie's life we see how parents' love affects children, who become parents, who pass the love to more families and to distant lands and to different people and to a broken society. Each loving union becomes part of the fabric of human relationships that God uses to weave his love into the lives of others. The next chapters explore these dynamics, showing how the love husband and wife share extends to and through others to fulfill God's purposes. The key principle is that the love of Christ expressed between parents is the most powerful instrument for multiplying Christ's love through our families. Spiritually healthy marriages are God's primary means of producing spiritually healthy children. As we represent Christ to one another, he becomes real in our homes, dear to our children, and powerful in the lives our families touch.

7

PARENTAL FOUNDATIONS

I WAS STAYING IN the home of a pastor, a man well known for scholarship and the significance of his church. As a conference speaker, I spent the afternoons working on evening messages. The pastor let me use the office in his home for my preparations. One afternoon, I could not help overhearing the sounds of children playing outside the window. But "playing" is not really a good description. One child, the nine-year-old son of the pastor, was dominating the others with cruelty, profanity, and intimidation.

The son's performance was hard to listen to and even harder to study through, so after a while I walked out of the office to take a break. The room opened at the bottom of a stairway. As I passed the stairs, a movement at the second-floor landing caught my eye. I glanced up to see the boy's mother watching him out a window overlooking the yard. She was a silhouette against the window. The light against the dark outline of her body made her posture a poignant picture of obvious pain. With shoulders drooped and head down, she flinched at the latest profanity from her son. Then she heard me too, and as she turned to face me, I realized she was crying.

From where I stood, the mother knew I had heard her child, and through her tears she said, "I don't know what's wrong with my son. His father doesn't know either. Somehow we have failed. Our son is only nine years old, and we have already failed. We just don't know what we should do."

The mother was near despair. Yet hidden in her words was an acknowledgment that still beaconed a biblical hope. The mother said, "*We* don't know what *we* should do." Though they were unsure what course they should take, this husband and wife still recognized an obligation rested on them. Despite their child's antics and the aching he was causing them, these parents acknowledged they still were responsible for their child's nurture.

This is the essence of biblical parenting: not acquiescing to children's wills but equipping them to live according to God's will. Sometimes this parental service is pleasant and other times painful, but it is always characterized by the self-less application of one's resources, wisdom, and energies to help a child grow in the knowledge and likeness of Christ. All aspects of biblical parenting—including training, nurture, and discipline—seek to serve these spiritual interests of the child.

Selfless parenting requires fathers and mothers to pour *themselves* into the welfare of their children. Parents who raise children according to God's standards do not pass the primary responsibility for their children to other adults; they do not pass the responsibility to other institutions, even the church; they do not pass the responsibility to the child—they do not take a "pass" on the responsibility. Parental responsibility for children is a personal duty to God and it cannot be passively fulfilled. Parents obedient to Scripture actively submit themselves to God in nurturing their children as his Word directs.

The apostle puts the responsibility for child rearing squarely on parents:

> Children, obey your parents in the Lord, for this is right. "Honor your father and mother"—which is the first commandment with a promise—"that it may go well with you and that you may enjoy long life on the earth." Fathers, do not exasperate your children; instead, bring them up in the training and instruction of the Lord.
>
> Ephesians 6:1–4

As simple as these words appear, parents in that decadent culture may have been tempted to a bit of exasperation with Paul. The words of instruction are so few! Only one sentence gives any direct instruction to parents. And, as a further complication, this sentence is addressed only to fathers.

Surely parents in New Testament times were not unlike us in wanting a healthy selection of child-rearing manuals. How could anyone in that age of rampant ungodliness raise children with so little guidance? Parents in this age ask the same question. With all the perils facing our children, and with all the consequent questions facing us, why does the Bible say so little? The answer lies in the building blocks undergirding these few words of parental instruction. The Bible's instruction to parents follows other instructions for the larger Christian household. Through the relationships that form the context for the family, the Lord gives parents much guidance for rearing children in his care.

A Love Relationship with the Lord—
the First Building Block

Paul's instruction to parents flows from a larger discussion of how the church should operate. This means the Lord expects biblical parenting to occur in a church context. We can learn much about parenting in the church—through the preaching of the Word, the example of elders, and the advice of other Christian parents. When my wife and I were first-time parents, we took many cues from other families we respected in the church.

Beyond these practical implications, however, there is a more fundamental reason why the Bible teaches parenting in a church context. God's true church is made up of those whose hearts are committed to him (see Eph. 3:16–21). The formal relationship one has with a church should be indicative of one's personal relationship with Christ. This means that a deep, personal relationship with the Lord is the most basic building block of Christian parenting. A Christian parent's first and most important priority is to love Jesus.

To sense the importance of God's love for good parenting, consider how Paul begins his instruction to Christian

> **Kathy's thought:** One of the most valuable Sunday school classes we have attended was one on Christian parenting. Many adult Sunday school classes are divided into age groups, but this one was composed of all ages—parents of infants, parents of teens, parents of grown children—and that was so helpful. We spent hours discussing parenting issues and ideas, each set of parents learning from the experience and wisdom of the others. I understand that roughly 50 percent of children in the United States now grow up without both their biological parents, and many more parents wonder how to raise children. Christian parents need each other for mutual training and encouragement.

households: "Be imitators of God, therefore, as dearly loved *children* and live a life of love, just as Christ loved us and gave himself up for us" (Eph. 5:1–2, italics mine). We learn how to love others by understanding how God loves us as his children. His love for us is the pattern for the way we should love, therefore our children directly benefit from our understanding of God's parental care.

To prepare us for parental care, Paul expresses God's love in parental terms many times. Even his opening greeting stresses God's parental love:

> Grace and peace to you from God our *Father* and the Lord Jesus Christ. Praise be to the God and *Father* of our Lord Jesus Christ, who has blessed us in the heavenly realms with every spiritual blessing in Christ. For he chose us in him before the creation of the world to be holy and blameless in his sight. In love he predestined us to be *adopted* as his *sons* through Jesus Christ, in accordance with his pleasure and will.
>
> Ephesians 1:2–5, italics mine

These words demonstrate Paul's zeal to root our parental practices in a solid understanding of our heavenly Father's love. There are at least two reasons that a relationship with God is a necessary foundation for biblical parenting. The first relates to parents' need for a *model*, and the second to our need for *security*.

Our Heavenly Model

We tend to become our parents. For good or ill, parental models shape us. Abusers raise abusers, alcoholics raise alcoholics, well-adjusted parents raise well-adjusted children. Of course there is comfort in this equation only if you are on the positive side. Fear and despair press in, however, if you recognize your own parents' modeling was inadequate. How can we hope to raise our children well if our own models are broken? The words of the apostle comfort *Christian* parents by reminding them that they have a positive model.

The Father of all Christians is God. The passage quoted above says God is "our Father." The grace in this simple statement is profound. The truth that God is our Father frees us from our past. Because we have a heavenly parent, we are not bound to the negative patterns and practices of our earthly parents. We are not destined to repeat their errors because theirs is not the only imprint on us. God provides us with another parental model—himself.

The heavenly Father's love can be more real, more powerful, more motivating than biology and learned behavior. An intimate relationship with him does more to establish what we will be as parents than any other factor in our background. The realization that *the Father we perceive our God to be largely shapes the parent we are able to be* challenges us to make sure that our understanding of our God is biblical.

Our Heavenly Security

The apostle says God has been our Father since before the creation of the world, reinforcing the security we need to parent well (see Eph. 1:4–5). Our greatest failings as parents typically result from our insecurities. I recognize this when I confess what upsets me most with my children. What makes me angriest? Too often it is what my children do that embarrasses me. In such moments I find that I too readily discipline out of concern for my reputation rather than out of concern for my child. At the root of such discipline is a fear of rejection. Beneath my anger is the fear that others will not think highly of me—that I will be relegated to the sidelines of their acceptance.

Conversely, it is often difficult for my wife (and for many other women) to discipline because of fear that a child will reject her. Fear of a child getting angry, turning a cold shoulder, or spurning love has stifled many a mom's discipline—and stirred many a child's rebellion.

Of course these are not gender-specific traits. There are plenty of fathers who will not discipline for fear of a child's rejection and many mothers who serve their own egos through managing the performance of their children. The point is *not* that both mothers and fathers have flaws but that insecurity affects our behavior. If we are more concerned about how others view us, we tend to overreact in discipline. If we are more concerned about how our children view us, we tend to underreact in discipline.

The sum of these truths is that anxious parents do not make good parents. So the Bible deals with the source of our anxieties with the assurance that God has dearly loved us since before the world

Kathy's thought: Yes, it has been hard for me to discipline in the face of my child's anger or rejection of me. At some point, however, I came to the realization that my love for my child must be greater than my enjoyment of his good humor; my love must be more stubborn than his mood; my love must be so unconditional that it will survive his rejection.

A friend once related to me her daughter Sherrie's frustration and anger over her parents' refusal to let her attend a classmate's party. The parents knew much more than their daughter about this classmate's family situation; they knew the party was not a good place for their girl to be. "I can take care of myself!" Sherrie protested. "Everyone else gets to go!" (You would think teenagers could come up with better arguments than the ones I used back then!) Sherrie's mom was tired of trying to reason with her child. Finally she took Sherrie by the shoulders, looked her square in the eyes, and said, "Sherrie, God made me the gate through which everything has to pass before it reaches you. I will do everything—anything—I can to keep you from getting hurt." I like that. God made me the gate.

began. Once this assurance takes root in a parent's heart, concern for self ceases to be the driving motive behind our parenting. Security in our relationship with God frees us to parent for our children's good—sharing our security with them rather than taking it from them (see Eph. 5:2).

A Love Relationship with a Spouse— the Second Building Block

The need to parent from security further explains why Paul talks about spouses before parents (see Eph. 5:22–33). He is concerned for more than biological order. His words establish a relational priority. My relationship with my wife should so confirm her security with the Lord that she has confidence to do what is best for our children, even if her decision risks a child's acceptance of her. My wife's relationship with me should so reinforce my security with the Lord that I do not need to discipline to protect my ego.

A healthy marriage supplies the spiritual support that allows discipline to be given primarily out of love for the child rather than the interests of either parent. God pours his love for children through parents whose priorities have developed within a context of personal security. The love parents share for each other enables them to love their children as God desires.

The Bible says much about how husbands and wives love before saying a little about how they should parent (see Eph. 5:22–33). The implicit message is that a healthy marriage relationship fosters biblical parenting. This does not mean that single parents cannot do a good job of raising children. God can provide grace for special needs in all kinds of homes dedicated to him, but single parenting is not the regular pattern of Scripture. God desires tightly bonded parents for more than having a united front for discipline (though such shoulder-to-shoulder responses are an important indication to a child of parental unity). More important is what parental unity accomplishes.

Teaching Commitment

Through the union of a man and a woman that a healthy marriage nurtures, a child learns a healthy pattern of intimacy, not just with another person but with God. What, after all, is the ultimate goal of a wife's submission to her husband's authority and a husband's sacrifice for his wife's glory? The ultimate aim is to bring the reality of Christ's love into the marriage. As parents enable each other to know and love Christ more, they also establish patterns of intimacy that teach children how to open their hearts to their family and their Lord.

Kathy's thought: When I was a child, a favorite game at school was Red Rover. We would get a large number of friends to play, then divide into two teams and form two parallel lines facing one another.

The kids in each line would link hands, then one from the first group would sing out to the other, "Red Rover, Red Rover, let Suzy come over!" Suzy would let go of her friends' hands and then run as fast and hard as she could into the opposing line. If the children in the first group were holding on to one another very securely, poor Suzy had no chance of breaking through the line. If, however, she blasted her way into a weak link, the chain was broken, and Suzy got to take a friend from that line and return triumphantly to her team.

When a husband and wife parent shoulder to shoulder, hands clasped firmly together, then let Suzy come over! Suzy will find in her parents two people who love and respect one another and who are united in their desire to do what is best for her.

Expressions of love for one another in the home are a direct path to understanding God's love. The greatest earthly gift a parent can give a child is a loving marriage. We will not submit or sacrifice adequately until we sense truly the consequences of marital failure for our children.

The impact of the parents' marriage on a child's nurture was painfully acknowledged by a Christian brother who shared his life's story with me. Raised in a large family, he says that a line of spiritual and emotional health seems to be drawn in the sand of time separating the older children from the younger. Emotional health, solid marriages, and spiritual maturity characterize the older children raised in the early, healthy years of his parents' marriage. Conversely, troubled psyches, brushes with the law, and spiritual indifference mark the younger children raised while the marriage was deteriorating. No one can prove a direct cause and effect for the differences. Healthy marriages do not guarantee well-adjusted children, and healthy children sometimes emerge from the unhealthiest home environments. Still, Scripture affirms what our instincts say: healthy children spring from the soil of healthy marriages.

Kathy's thought: I hope that, if our children were to be asked their strongest impressions of their parents, they would say—in this order—that we each love Jesus with all our heart, and that we love each other more than anything on this earth. A friend of Bryan's expresses her experience this way: "I never doubted my parents' love for one another—never. They clearly loved one another—and me—unconditionally. As a result, I was able early on to believe that God loves me unconditionally. Understanding grace was not a hard thing for me, because I grew up with it all around me."

This conclusion is not merely anecdotal. In a sampling of students at a prestigious university, almost half cited their parents' divorce as their "most determinative life-changing event."[1] The stories and statistics of these future leaders join with Scripture to testify that safeguarding the marriage relationship remains an essential element of parenting. The relationship between parents is a primary conduit of God's grace into a family.

A parent who slights his or her spouse for career advancement, unnecessary economic advantage, or personal fulfillment hurts the family. There are eternal consequences for selfish gain bought at the expense of a healthy home. Not even the pursuit of ministry at the expense of a family will serve God's purposes, since ministries are destroyed by broken families.

For the good of a child, the love of one's spouse must take precedence even over the relationship of the parent with that child. A parent who pours affection and attention into children at the expense of honoring a spouse may seem to be serving the children, but such priorities actually jeopardize their welfare. Because God intends for the parents' relationship to bring the reality of Christ's love into the home, a spouse who sacrifices the marriage—even out of apparent concern for the child—jeopardizes the spiritual understanding of that child. When the parents' love for each other takes a backseat to any earthly concern—even a child—the child's ability to know the character of the heavenly Father is injured.

The Bible does not encourage parents to slight their children for selfish enjoyments. Yet parents who can't find time and ways to appreciate each other deprive their children of the loving example they need. Christian parents need to make goo-goo eyes at one another occasionally. It's good for the kids. The Bible simply will not permit a husband and wife to neglect each other by directing the love that God intends for their spouse to their child.

A loving relationship with God and a loving relationship with a spouse form the foundation of biblical parenting. When we assume the responsibilities of parents, we subject ourselves to the consequences of these truths. This means we honor God and our spouse for the sake of children even when such commitments prove to be trying and difficult.

Giving Comfort

Understanding that parenting grows out of relationships can give us needed comfort. The Bible's emphases show that the daily context of Christian living is the most powerful tool of child rearing. God does not prescribe a precise set of right or wrong parental habits. A child's nurture is not determined by a list of rules mysteriously divined from Scripture's few statements on parenting.

This conclusion flies in the face of some Christian teaching that there is only one correct way to affirm or show affection or discipline. Some have even claimed biblical proof for the proper feeding times of infants. Such instructions deny the liberties of Scripture and the dignity of individual differences. Such teaching also seems to imply that we are likely to ruin our children if we make a single mistake in some particular moment or aspect of a child's upbringing. This is precisely what Scripture does *not* attest.

We all make mistakes as parents. This does not automatically make us bad parents. My wife and I have made mistakes with our children. There have been times of improper discipline, impatience, and poor judgment that I hope God will erase from their minds. But if they remember, I won't despair. Scripture does not require me to believe that momentary error will wreck my children. Were I to believe it could, then I would become paralyzed, fearing to do anything that might forever ruin them. I might also refuse ever to examine my parenting practices lest I have to confess that I had warped my children by past mistakes.

Because God places the foundations for biblical child rearing in a spiritual- and marital-relationship context, no single act of well-intentioned parenting is determinative of a child's future. The grace that a Christian heart embraces and that a Christian's marriage should foster allows Christian parents the privilege to fail, to seek forgiveness, and to try again. The Father's unconditional, eternal love erases the dread that a mistake in action or judgment will ruin our children. This grace of God frees Christians to parent without second-guessing every act of discipline or feeling the need to deny past errors.

When one of our sons was a freshman in college, he was diagnosed with a chronic and sometimes debilitating disease. Within weeks of that diagnosis one of his very good friends died suddenly and tragically. Then, in driving to the funeral of that friend, my son's car was hit and totaled by a speeding teen who ran a red light. With so much weighing on him, my son was as low emotionally as we have ever known. We were terribly worried for him but knew also that parents can be the last people a nineteen-year-old young man desires for counsel. We prayed, of course, but still needed help in caring for our son. The one who came to our rescue and our son's aid was his college minister. He was a young man I had taught in seminary and whose family my wife had loved for many years. This young minister gave his time, his wisdom, and his heart in helping my son through that very difficult time.

Kathy's thought: I cannot say how often I have needed the reassurances in this paragraph. Many times when our children were young, I would crawl into bed at the end of the day and cry. "All I did today was spank!" I would weep to my husband. "Will they ever remember me *not* scolding?" My dear husband would put his arms around me and assure me over and over that, yes, they *will* remember the delightful times (you do, don't you, Colin? Jordan? Corinne? Katy?), and that if I did indeed spank that day, then they must have needed it and would be better for it the next day.

Sometimes, though, we did make mistakes; we did spank or scold too quickly; we did make decisions that we later regretted and for which we had to apologize. But through it all, and above all, we believe in the Holy Spirit. We believe God works in our hearts and in the hearts of our children. And ultimately all we can do is our prayerful best, then trust God to guide us, forgive us, and strengthen us for the next day.

In reflecting on those hard days, we have understood more of how important and broad are the foundations God lays to enable Christians to parent as he desires. Kathy's and my love were the foundation of care for our son, but that love was also a link to other parents, children, and church leaders who contributed to his care in ways we alone could not. The Lord laid a foundation that even crossed generations as one I taught became God's instrument in helping the son we love. As we reflect on the way the Lord constructed our lives to provide care beyond what we could manage or express, we marvel at the intricacies of his wisdom and mercy, and we even more highly treasure the foundations that he lays for our family's welfare.

8

PARENTAL RESPONSIBILITIES

MY PREADOLESCENT SONS had invited a friend to come with us for a weekend trip at a cabin in the woods. The friend was from a broken home and it showed. My sons were both shocked and fascinated by his crude speech, rebellious behavior, skilled lying, and vulgar humor.

One afternoon I listened from the next room as a particularly vulgar comment was made and my sons roared with laughter. I entered the room and asked what the laughter was all about. One of my sons then lied and told me that the laughter was about another joke. I saw red. I was prepared for a visiting kid to misbehave and lie, but I was not about to let my own son get away with such. I asked him again what the laughter was about, and again he lied. With one hand I took his arm to lead him into the woods, and with the other hand I grabbed a child's canoe paddle with the intention of using it on my son's canoe end until he told me the truth.

Neither of us made it far into the woods. My son sensed my rage and instead of resisting me, he began to groan in a way that I had never heard before: "Oh no, oh noooo." It pains me even now to remember the sound. I realized I had gone too far. My willingness to embarrass my son in front of his friend, to put him in a position where he had difficulty doing anything but lie (a position I strive to keep from putting my children in), and then to take something to spank him (something I had never done before)—all told my son that this discipline was not about helping him, it was about venting my steam. I stopped in my tracks, told my son that I had been more wrong than he, and promised never again to threaten him with a paddle. We went back to the camp both sobered by the experience and relatively sure that neither would repeat our errors that weekend.

Now that he's grown up, I have asked my son if he remembers that day of my rage. I am thankful that he does not. But I do remember, and sometimes I still wonder what snapped in me that day and what I might have done had not the Holy Spirit used my son's fear to douse the heat in my smoldering heart. My mistake was serious enough to sear itself in my memory for many years, but the Lord used many more influences to shape my son's heart and mind so that this single event was not determinative of his future or mine.

The Responsibilities of the Child—
the Third Building Block (continued from chapter 7)

God provides us great comfort in reassuring us that we can make mistakes and still be good parents, but that does *not* mean that God releases us from responsibility. God's Word describes the responsibilities that should accompany the relationships of both parents and children.

What does God expect children to do? The simple answer is that he expects them to obey (see Eph. 6:1).

The Bible tells children to submit to their parents "in the Lord." This means that a child should do whatever parents require so long as their instruction is not contrary to God's will. Scripture also makes it clear that this submission is about more than just *doing* what a parent requires. Sullen, angry, begrudging fulfillment of duty is not acceptable. An obedient child must also *honor* father and mother (see Eph. 6:2). Children must submit in action and attitude to their parents' instruction.

Submission Is Right

The apostle Paul supplies two reasons for a child's submission. First, children are to obey, "for this is right" (Eph. 6:1). What a peculiarly simple and, at first glance, unnecessary statement. Despite our temptation to retort, "Of course," there is great significance in the apostle's simple affirmation. We sense the significance when we wonder whether to make our children obey.

Consider that moment when a little three-year-old bundle of sugar and spice, bedecked in the finery of a new Easter dress, ignores her daddy's "No" and grabs a handful of candy intended for guests. Then, when Daddy patiently tells this precious package of lace and sweetness to put the candy back, she says, "No." Now, Daddy knows that if he does anything about this rebellion, he will feel like the Grinch who stole Easter. What should this father require?

What does the Bible say? Children, obey your parents, *for this is right.*

Because God knows that we parents are easily torn by our love for our children and our insecurities about ourselves, he speaks plainly. Require your children to obey, he says, "for this is right." When a young mother cannot bring herself to discipline her child, when a father will not provide the attention to discipline, when the latest child-rearing book makes us question whether we should just ignore our children's outbursts—in each of these moments we need the simplicity of Scripture.

> **Kathy's thought:** I have often justified requiring my children to obey by reminding myself—and them—that it is not only right to obey, but it is *best.* "If you are in danger," I have told them, "I need you to obey me *right now.* If you are about to cross the street, and I see a car is coming and I say, 'Stop,' you need to stop. You need to obey *right now,* without question or conversation, because to disobey is dangerous."
>
> As a parent, I want my child to be safe from all kinds of danger, not just approaching cars. My child needs to obey me because God has given me the job of protecting her from danger and guiding her away from sin—guiding her into not only a safe place but also a place where her heart is following a safe path.

Yes, there are moments when our circumstances will require discretion regarding the timing and degree of discipline. Still, we cannot make lack of discipline a pattern. If we think we love our children too much to require them to do what is right, then we really have not loved them enough.

Submission Is Good

The apostle explains the relationship between loving our children and disciplining them with the second reason children should submit to their parents. Not only is it right for our children to obey, it is good for them (see Eph. 6:2–3). God promises obedient children *blessing* ("that it may go well with you") and *safekeeping* ("that you may enjoy long life on earth").

The statement about long life does not guarantee that obedience will ward off all disease and accidents. It is a general promise of well-being that accompanies the fifth of the Ten Commandments, telling children to obey. (Note, however, that the promise also has a literal fulfillment in that children who honor God with their lives will be kept safe eternally.) In essence, the apostle warns that a disobedient child endangers himself physically and spiritually.

The dangers of disobedience were well demonstrated to my family on a long-ago trip to an amusement park. We were waiting in line for a train ride. As the wait lengthened, a five- or six-year-old child in front of us decided to climb on a fence railing. His position made it hard for the remaining people in line to pass. His mother reacted quickly, saying, "Johnny, come down from there." Johnny did not move even an eyelash.

A litany of parental attempts at correction followed. Had the damage being done to the child's character not been so evident, these attempts would have been comical:

"Johnny, come down from there, right now!

"Johnny, come down. I won't tell you again.

"Johnny, I am going to count to three. One, two, . . . two and a half. . . . Now, Johnny, I mean it.

"Johnny, I am going to tell your father when we get home.

"Okay, Johnny, just stay there. I'm going to leave you if you don't come down.

"Johnny, please, please come down. I'll buy you an ice cream cone."

We squeezed by the child when it was our turn to ride the train, but for all we know Johnny is now twenty years old and still sitting on that fence rail.

If you can re-create that incident in your mind's eye, think not only of the stone-cold look on Johnny's face. Consider the countenance of the surrounding people. What do their faces reflect? They are all frowning at the child. Responsible parents must dare to look at these faces because they prophesy the future of an uncontrolled child. A child who will not obey a parent's authority will see only the world's frown.

Not only does such an undisciplined child inherit a parent's frustration, he also reaps the disapproval of teachers, neighbors, other parents, friends, future employers, and ultimately his own heart. A child who consistently sees his reflection in the frown of the world can only view himself as despised. This is why the book of Proverbs says that parents who will not discipline hate their child (see 13:24). Such parenting subjects a child to a lifetime of misery—a fate we would want only for our enemies.

A disobedient child is a bother to the world and also a danger to himself. In a nearby park I witnessed a child racing away from his father, who was frantically calling, "Jason, don't run that way!"

"Why, Daddy?" asked Jason as he kept running, and then he tumbled headlong into a concrete culvert.

The child's bloodied forehead was a vivid object lesson of Scripture's truth. We require obedience from children because it is right for them and it is good for them. Obedience protects children

> **Kathy's thought:** I have been among the frowners. Who hasn't seen the wild child in the grocery store and glared in his direction? Recognition of our own attitudes toward unruly children should fuel our resolve to train and discipline firmly and consistently.
>
> I have driven my children and their friends to many field trips in the course of raising four kids, and I remember one in particular. Luke was a classmate of one of our sons, and Luke gave me fits all day long. I had never before that day had to pull the car off the road, turn around, and glare at a child and say, "You may not use that language in my car!" And this was to a first-grader! As I turned around to pull back onto the highway, my blood still boiling, I suddenly recalled my husband's words: "A child who will not obey a parent's authority will see only the world's
>
> *continues...*

from consequences that are both earthly and eternal, for ultimately a child who does not know obedience cannot know the Lord.

The Responsibilities of the Parent— the Fourth Building Block

The fourth building block in the foundation of child rearing is parental obedience. Simply stated, *parents* are to raise their children. The Bible provides an implicit understanding of who does the child raising. Fathers and mothers are those given parenting instructions (see Eph. 6:2–4), not grandparents, not babysitters or siblings, not institutions outside the home. This does not mean the Bible forbids parents ever to utilize the services of others. Still, the words of Scripture challenge all parents to make sure they are the *chief* caregivers.

frown." My heart broke at that moment for Luke, and I resolved two things: to love Luke, and to renew my loving discipline of my own children, so that they might never see the frown of the world because of their disobedient hearts.

If I love my child the way I say I do, then I will do anything to keep him from harm. If that harm is a patch of poison ivy or a swarm of angry hornets, I will guide him away from those dangers. If that harm is the disapproval and rejection of those around him because of his disobedience, then I must keep him from that too.

Social, economic, and spiritual pressures are tearing parents from their home responsibilities. Too many parents have turned over the upbringing of their children to day care, school care, church care, grandparents, or nannies. Economic necessities or family exigencies may well force parents to child care they may not prefer. Life is not always served in *Leave It to Beaver* packages. But for our children's future, we must examine whether genuine necessity justifies the time our children spend away from us.

I want to emphasize that no one unfamiliar with the complexities facing your family has a right to determine that you automatically sin by using any nonparental care system. The question of who is raising your child is determined by the degree of conscientious involvement you invest in your child's nurture. This is not a matter of putting a stopwatch on the hours a child spends here or there. Nevertheless, when a husband and wife work long hours in demanding jobs that make them both exhausted as they pick up kids from Grandma's or day care, then they must question whether they are obeying the Bible. Bigger homes, nicer cars, and longer vacations, purchased at the price of absent parents, cost our children far too much. Scripture values our families far more.

Parenting is a spiritual discipline. This shows in the wording the apostle Paul uses to instruct parents. Paul addresses only "fathers" (Eph. 6:4). This is not because the apostle thinks mothers have no role in child rearing. He identifies the mother's importance when he tells children to "honor your father and mother" (6:2). By directly addressing the spiritual head of the home, though, the apostle underscores the spiritual challenge of parenting. Because the head of the home is accountable, the task has spiritual priority. While a man needs help in child rearing, he cannot delegate all decisions and activities to an-

> **Kathy's thought:** Often the bigger homes or nicer cars aren't the only issue. Priorities may be well placed, yet the realities of the family situation dictate hard choices. For many years I served as music director at our church, and for many of those years that worked well for our family. The church was (initially) small, the choir was small, and almost all of my choir work was easily accomplished while the kids were in school. Choir practice was on a night when the kids' youth activities took place. But the church grew during those years, and so did our kids. Suddenly we found ourselves with three teens, an elementary school daughter, and Mom working way too many hours outside the home.
>
> After much prayer and long talks with my husband, I retired from my choir job. It was hard, because I had enjoyed the work very much and loved being so involved in worshiping the Lord through music. But it was also absolutely the right decision, and one the Lord affirmed again and again. It was the right season to focus on my soon-to-be-in-college children and to turn my gifts more toward nurturing the nest.

other. A father remains biblically responsible for the nurture of his children.

In Paul's writings, *father* most often refers to God. This word echo should help men understand that we are to nurture our children as God fathers us. He willingly offers his presence and care to nurture us. Such fathering is in short supply in our society. News specials have recently shifted the blame for our nation's inner-city problems from drugs to the absence of fathers. But the fathering crisis is not limited to poor neighborhoods. In that sampling of university students already cited (see chapter 7), only one mentioned a father when asked the factors contributing most to molding their lives.[1]

At all rungs of society fathers have led in parental abdication.[2] The Bible leads parents back to their homes through the headship of fathers. Scripture's specific words remind us that parenting is a priority for both mother *and* father.

Having laid the foundation of relationships and responsibilities, the apostle finally turns our attention to the actual practices of Christian parents (see Eph. 6:4). We are told what not to do, and then what to do.

What Parents Should *Not* Do — the Fifth Building Block

The Bible says, "Do not exasperate your children" (Eph. 6:4). In the Old Testament *exasperate* (in the Greek translation of Paul's time) does not refer simply to frustration. The term describes God's own just anger over Israel's idolatry. Exasperation refers to a righteous resentment of actions or attitudes inconsistent with one's faith commitments. Thus an exasperated child is one who has a right to be upset because of inconsistencies between a parent's stated beliefs and actual behaviors.

Our children have a right to be upset with us when our actions conflict with our spiritual values. We do not have to guess the values the apostle has in mind. Preceding verses stress using authority based on the example of Christ, expressing love patterned after the sacrifice of Christ, and showing respect out of reverence for Christ. What would be inconsistent with these values that would cause exasperation in children?

> *Authority that contradicts its own standards*, as when a mother tells a child to quit whining by whining at him, or when a father compels self-control by throwing a temper tantrum.
>
> *Love that requires sacrifice but seeks self*, as when a mother pushes for a child's success to affirm her own worth, or when a father punishes to enforce behavior that serves his own reputation or convenience.
>
> *Respect demanded at the expense of individual dignity*, as when a mother shames a child into obedience, or when a father exerts control by comparing the child with others inside or outside the family.

Whether discipline takes the form of manipulative guilt trips, shaming silent treatments, or abusive denials of a child's worth, the home that rules by condemnation undermines biblical obedience. We are dispensers of God's grace into our children's lives. Our children should learn to identify and reverence God's character through the way we treat them, both in moments of profound pride and in times of intense disappointment.

When one of my children was younger, I struggled to apply these truths. My son bordered on being hyperactive. I was unprepared to deal with a child who seemed oblivious to our expectations and also unconcerned about his own safety.

We used lots of traditional discipline—methods that worked with our other children—to try to coerce our son's obedience. I sometimes found myself spanking him three, four, or more times a day in attempts to gain control of him, but to my dismay my efforts failed.

No amount of correction changed him. His misconduct threatened to demoralize the whole family. As a result, I found I sometimes disciplined out of the fury I felt over my own failure. His behavior challenged my own sense of parental adequacy. Even worse, he began to think of himself as a "wild" child because I spoke about him that way. My concern for my own reputation was robbing my son of my love, his dignity, and God's grace.

Something had to change. One day I said to my wife, "I can't spank him anymore." This was as much an admission of my failure as it was a decision to try something else. Stubborn adherence to discipline measures that had worked with other children—measures that were part of my own background and demanded the least change in me—had, in fact, driven me from what I knew Christian parenting required. I was damaging my son to prove my parental competence.

We began to consider alternatives. Still, we knew abandoning discipline was not biblically permissible. God was gracious. First, he brought into my wife's choir a child development expert who told us that in their developing years, brilliant children (such as our son) are often hyperactive. Their actions result not from intentional disobedience but from their brains' demands for new sources of information and stimuli. Second, the Lord helped us recall that even in our child's most excitable moments, he would almost always settle when his mother took him into her lap, stroked his hair, and told him about how thrilled we were the day God brought him into our world. If we could just capture the dynamics of that calming mechanism, we thought we might have a new discipline tool.

For the next several months whenever control was needed, instead of spanking we simply made our son sit down. He had to stop and be still until we said he could resume his activity. For this active child such time-outs were almost torture, but we insisted. The technique did *not* work like a charm, but over a period of weeks we began to see results. By allowing him to decompress, instead of overloading his system with the additional stimulation of a spanking, our son gained control.

In hindsight I feel foolish when I consider the mistakes I made. Yet confession of these errors gives me a greater appreciation for Scripture's wisdom and God's grace. By insisting that my son respond to a single kind of discipline in the same manner as his siblings, I was not allowing him the dignity of being the individual God made him. The Lord has developed my son into a special person. I am very proud of the spiritual maturity in his life. Yet I recognize that I could have greatly damaged the understanding of God's grace in him if the Lord had not made my errors apparent.

Godly parenting should reflect a deep understanding of our Lord's grace. Out of respect for the individual gifts God has granted my children, I must submit myself to the responsibility of discovering ways to discipline them that honor the unique ways God has made them. Biblical parenting requires me to respect the dignity of my children's differences and to affirm their worth without seeking to inflate mine.

As my children have grown older and their maturing involves more complex issues, I have discovered how important it is simply to resolve to love them—and to express my resolve even when we differ. More and more I realize that my parenting must remain consistent with my understanding of the grace God extends to me. I must not exasperate my children by disciplining for my sake (rather than theirs). Grace requires that I respect the unique ways God has made and is maturing each of them.

> **Kathy's thought:** I'm sure I'm not the only mom who has ached for the child in the grocery store as her mom shouts at her, "You drive me crazy! You are so stupid! Get out of my way!" and so on. In our household we have words or phrases that are forbidden in addressing one another: stupid, idiot, liar, worthless, and—the ultimate—"I hate you." We have made the decision that we will not ever demean one another in these ways. Bryan and I will not use these words to one another or to our children, and our children may not say them to each other (or to us—as if they would ever dare!). We do not and, by God's grace, will not say to a child, "You are a bad boy (or girl)." These kinds of words have no place in addressing an individual we believe the Lord of the universe put into our lives for us to nurture and raise in his image.

What Parents Should Do—
the Sixth Building Block

God does not tell us merely *what not to do* for our children. He tells us *what to do* as well. Christian parents should "bring them [children] up in the training and instruction of the Lord" (Eph. 6:4). The great theologian John Calvin translated this "bring them up" phrase as "let them [children] be fondly cherished." This interpretation reflects how the Bible uses these nurturing terms elsewhere. Paul uses similar wording earlier when he says a husband should cherish his wife as much as he "cares" for his own body and just as Christ does the church (5:29). Paul now intensifies these concepts in his instruction to fathers. The effect is that each father must care for his child as much as he "cares" for his own flesh.

As the first husband, Adam, "cared" for his wife as flesh of his flesh; and as Christ "cares" for his bride, the church (the product of his sacrificed flesh), so we as parents are to "care" intensely for our children. Ordinarily, they are the product of our flesh. Since our life is in them, we are to bring up our children with the care we give to our own bodies. We nurture our children as the essence of our lives. The physical and spiritual vitality God grants us should also thrive in our children through our sacrificial care. Parents are givers. We pour Christ's love into the nurture of those he commits to our care.

How do we nurture with such care? The apostle Paul gives two words to guide: *training* and *instruction*. These terms have slightly different shades of meaning. *Training* carries the positive connotation—parents are to model, teach, and encourage godly patterns of life. *Instruction* contains a negative nuance—parents are to warn, correct, and discipline when actions or attitudes are inconsistent with godliness. The shades of meaning may be clearer in older translations that encourage parents to raise children "in the *nurture* and *admonition* of the Lord." These words describe caring guidance and loving reproof. They remind us that godly parenting requires a balance of affirmation and correction.

The scriptural instruction to provide a balance of firm guidance and loving correction finds almost startling corroboration in modern family research:

> Delinquents and criminals tend to come from homes in which discipline is *overstrict or erratic*, supervision is unsuitable, neither parent shows warmth or love, and there is little or no closeness of family members. Nondelinquents are more apt to come from homes in which discipline is *firm but kindly*, supervision is suitable, parents show affection for the child,

and the family does many things together [italics mine]. . . . Research in the area of child development shows that "firm but kindly" is optimal. Diana Baunrind (1970), in a ten year study of parent-child relationships, found that *authoritative* parenting in which the parent exerts firm control without hemming the child in with too many restrictions is more apt to produce a motivated, friendly, moral, and cooperative child than either *authoritarian* parenting in which the parent attempts to shape, control, and evaluate all the activities of the child, or *permissive* parenting in which few demands are placed upon the child who is permitted to do whatever he or she pleases. . . . The children of authoritarian parents tend to be discontented, distrustful, and lacking in warmth, while the children of permissive parents tend to be the least self-reliant and self-controlling of all three groups. Children reared permissively are often said to be spoiled and may become tyrants who rule over their own parents. . . .

Authoritative parents use a unique combination of high control and positive encouragement of the child's autonomy and independence. There is no question but that the parent is in charge. Guidelines and rules are given within which the child must operate, and standards for future conduct are set. But parents share their reasons for the rules and encourage verbal give-and-take on the part of the child. Both the rights and interests of the parents and the rights and interests of the child are taken into consideration.[3]

How do we achieve this balance of training and instruction, of affirmation and correction, of firm but kindly parenting? The answer lies in the final words of the apostle's instruction. We raise our children in the training and instruction "of the Lord." The chief goal of parenting is to enable children to know and honor God. This means we should constantly examine whether our words, our manner, our correction, and our home environment nurture an understanding of the Lord. This requires more than the application of a specific technique of discipline or setting a curfew in accord with the standards of the latest parenting seminar.

No single set of techniques or rules will make us good parents. Our sins and our children are far more perplexing than any book, seminar, or sermon can comprehensively cover. I am *not* devaluing the many helpful things that we can learn from Christian authors and other experienced parents. We simply must remember that the complexities of each child's nature will not allow cookie-cutter responses.

Kathy's thought: At about the same time our fourth child was born, there was some discussion among the young moms at church and at the seminary about the latest child-rearing book. The author's thesis was that an infant, from his or her earliest days, needs to be trained to live according to a strict schedule. Eating, sleeping, cuddling—all were to be carefully scheduled and planned according to the author's prescribed timetable, and the parents were instructed to follow this schedule precisely, regardless of whether the child was crying, sleeping, or so on. Now, as I said, our little one was our fourth, and any book that advocated waking a sleeping child to feed him or her earned my instant suspicion. More than one young mom came to me in tears, asking whether it really could be wrong to let her

continues...

Parenting by Grace

This uniqueness of each child should not frustrate or bewilder us. God has applied beautiful creativity to making each of our children special. Such creativity affirms individual dignity and drives Christian parents to tune their hearts to the Lord's purposes. A loving relationship with God is fundamental to Christian parenting. This is especially obvious when making discipline decisions. If we do not have a grip on grace, then we will not have the courage to discipline; but if grace has no grip on us, then there will be no constraint on our discipline.

Christian parenting compels us to reflect our Savior and as a consequence leads us to greater dependence on him. By submitting our interests to the good of children, we discover our own nobility and Christlikeness. News reports of the actions of two parents aboard Amtrak's Sunset Limited in 1993 revealed these truths with a powerful poignancy.

Gary and Mary Jane Chancey were riding on the Limited on a foggy September morning when the train plunged off a railway bridge into a bayou outside Mobile, Alabama. The Chanceys were traveling with their eleven-year-old daughter, Andrea, who had cerebral palsy and required a wheelchair. As their train car sank into the bayou, water rushed into the Chanceys' capsized compartment. Fighting the flow of water rushing through the window, the two parents combined their efforts to lift Andrea to a rescuer. Then the water pressure overwhelmed them, pushed them deep into the darkness of the train cabin, and they were gone.

These parents gave their lives to the purpose of lifting their child to physical safety. God calls all Christian parents to similar sacrifice, enduring what may be intense pressure and pain to lift our children to spiritual safety. We are not all called to die for our children, but we die to self each time—for our children's sake—we hold our tongues, control our anger, endure being misunderstood, take time for a ball game, absorb an insult, ignore an embarrassment, turn down a promotion requiring more time away, love patiently, discipline consistently, and forgive always. By the ways we

sleeping infant rest, or whether she really had to wait for the scheduled time to cuddle her baby!

My advice to these women was, and still is, to read the books on child rearing (especially by Christian authors), take a class on child development in order to learn how a child's mind grows and develops, and then listen to your own instincts. "Know your child," I have said. "Talk to your husband, pray, talk with Christian moms whose advice you value, and then trust yourself. Believe that God has made you the mother of this child to bond with him or her and to know this child's needs at a deeper level than any generic advice (as good as it may be) can offer."

love God and each other, by the ways we reflect the Lord and mold our children's perception of him, we enable our children to understand their Savior's love for them. In doing so, we discern the love we require as well as the love we must give. By lifting our children to the Savior, we become like him and thus discover in a parent's heart another means to measure and to reverence the love of the Savior who lifts us to heaven by his sacrifice.

9

EACH FOR THE OTHER
FOREVER

A FRIEND OF MINE works as an ethnolinguist—he studies cultures through the way they communicate. His scientific studies are very interesting but offer him little opportunity for wealth and stardom. He has had to learn to reconcile himself to these limitations.

When he was in graduate school, the lack of lucrative potential began to bother my friend so much that he would lie awake at night plotting how to turn his knowledge into profit. The apparent answer came at a school social.

Graduate students from throughout the university attended the party. This led to some good-natured sparring among those from different departments about the value of their respective career tracks. My friend fared poorly in the verbal competition because hardly anyone knew what an ethnolinguist was, and several doubted if this field of study truly had any real "science" behind it. Responding to a friendly challenge to prove the validity of his studies, my friend claimed that he could pick out the law students attending the party just by listening to their conversation. He succeeded! At the end of the party he had all of the lawyers-in-training fingered simply by the way they talked.

His success at the party crystallized my friend's plan for profit. He reasoned that since he could identify the speech pattern of lawyers, he should also be able to figure out how really successful lawyers talk. Then for fat fees he would teach this "successful speech" to attorneys hungry for their own career advancement. My friend was sure fame and fortune were right around the corner. His own studies soon convinced him otherwise.

He discovered that young lawyers and law students *sound* like lawyers. The most successful lawyers sound like *normal* people. The attorneys who really succeed depend on actions not words.

What is true of law is also true of love: those whose love succeeds depend on actions not words. That is really the core of the apostle John's message about our relationships. He writes:

> This is how we know what love is: Jesus Christ laid down his life for us. And we ought to lay down our lives for our brothers. If anyone has material possessions and sees his brother in need but has no pity on him, how can the love of God be in him? Dear children, let us not love with words or tongue but with actions and in truth.
>
> 1 John 3:16–18

The Problems with Words

The wisdom of the apostle echoes in our observations of marriages all around us. Merely saying the right words does not secure love. Everyone starts out saying the right words. All join in the familiar chorus:

"I love you."

"This is forever."

"I'll never forsake you."

Still, we know that saying these right words does not necessarily knit two lives together. The problem is not that people are dishonest in what they say. Almost no one lies when they repeat their vows of affection before the preacher. No one plans to have a miserable life. Everyone says, "I love you," and at that moment means it.

The problem is that couples cannot depend on words alone to keep them together. Words are too slippery. My wife and I went shopping for a washing machine a couple of years ago and discovered how words slip in meaning. We found out that if the capacity of a washer is listed as "large," that really means small. If washers are listed as "extra large," that means medium. Only washers with the words "super large" are actually large. The situation gets worse if you go looking for a mattress. The label "firm" means soft. The words "extra firm" signify kinda mushy. "Super firm" means only you're gettin' there. You do not find firm until you buy what our salesman called the "Imperial Superba-Firm II."

Words can also have different meanings for different people in their marriage commitments. For some "forever" means for a real long time. For others "till death do us part" means until our affections die. For some the promise to stay united "in sickness and in health" means as long as you don't make me too miserable for too long and the problems we face are not your fault.

It's not just that different people use the same words to mean different things. Our own words can change in meaning as our relationships change. A woman once told me how the words of her marriage changed, reflecting a changing relationship. She said, "When I was twenty-one, I cried when my husband said good-bye to go on a business trip, because I was so miserable when he was gone. When I was twenty-four, I cried when I heard him say hello, because I was so miserable when he was home. Before we were both thirty, I stopped crying and he stopped saying hello or good-bye, because I no longer cared whether he was home or gone."

Words are never enough to seal a love that lasts. The problem is *not* simply that we have difficulty calibrating the "forever" in the love that we promise each other. Our real challenge is defining the nature of the love that lasts. Words cannot adequately express this kind of love, much less secure it. The best poetry cannot encompass eternal love; our favorite song cannot really capture it; the most wonderful words inspired by feelings that we can hardly stand to breathe into sentences still do not say all that a ceaseless love must be. Words alone simply cannot

> **Kathy's thought:** I was recently sitting in the waiting room of the local mammography lab, awaiting my annual scan. A dozen or so women were there, all of us self-conscious in our little cotton robes and trying to concentrate on whatever magazine happened to be available, when into the room came an elderly gentleman. "Excuse me," he said to the nurse at the desk (and in that setting, a man's voice caught everyone's attention at once). "I'm here for my wife." "Yes, sir," the nurse responded, surprised. "Are you
>
> *continues...*

bear love's weight over time. What we say to each other, or even what we say to ourselves about our feelings for each other, cannot guarantee a love that will last.

The Need for Actions

What secures true love if words cannot? The apostle answers when he says not to love with lip service but "with actions and in truth" (1 John 3:18). There is no question about the type of actions John has in mind. He explains this in a previous verse where he offers his own definition of love: "This is how we know what love is: Jesus Christ laid down his life for us" (v. 16).

John defines love by sacrifice. The preeminent example he offers is that of Jesus who willingly gave up his glory and privileges to suffer on the cross for your good and mine. John goes on to say that "we ought to lay down our lives" for each other (v. 16), and he offers the concrete example of sharing our material possessions with those in need as embodying this type of love (see v. 17).

No mystery lies in applying these truths to marriage. The love that secures this most intimate of relationships must also

here to pick her up? What is her name?" "No, she's not here today," answered the man. "I'm here to make an appointment for her. My wife has Alzheimer's, and her doctor told us she probably has breast cancer too." All eyes in the room, and all our hearts, were now on this man. "The doctor wants her to have a mammogram," the husband continued, "and I know she'll be very frightened. I want you to show me what will happen to her, what it will be like for her. If I can tell her, if I can be with her, maybe she won't be so afraid."

Seemingly unaware that every woman in the room was now mesmerized by his words, he went on. "It's hard, you know, seeing her like this. Sometimes people ask me how I can go on, how I can keep taking care of her. I tell them, 'I love her. She's my wife. I took vows when we got married. I promised to love her forever, and I meant it.' So maybe if I can tell her, you know, what this will be like, maybe she won't be so afraid." This simple, unashamed expression of the man's unfailing devotion to his wife, even as she was losing her ability to respond to or even recognize it, moved every woman in the room to tears. The truth and power of his words were confirmed by sacrificial actions that spoke even more eloquently of unconditional, unwavering, and unending love—the kind of love that ennobles and secures our marriages.

be sacrificial. Of course God does not expect us physically to die for each other every day. We are, however, to die to self each day. The satisfaction of our own needs and desires cannot be the primary reason we enter, nor continue in, marriage. Such motives will never allow true love to flourish and endure.

An irony of this book on Christian marriage is that during its writing, my job has required that I be away from home more than at any other time in my marriage. Thus while I was writing about the need for each spouse to live for the other, the daily care of our home and children has fallen to Kathy with unprecedented weight. Upon her have fallen household chores, financial bookkeeping, children's discipline, carpooling, and innumerable social obligations that to describe as "wearying" would be a gross understatement.

Through all of this, Kathy has refused to complain and, instead, has been my support when I have come home exhausted and occasionally frustrated. She has had every right to resent the extra duties heaped on her and to trumpet the unfairness of my absences. Kathy could easily broker her sacrifices into greater concern for herself or less ministry for me. When friends have encouraged "pity parties" because of "the great sacrifice" that she is making, she has asserted her desire to support my ministry and the necessity of this current phase of my work. Kathy and I both have privately shed some tears of loneliness and weariness. We have both longed for more time together. Overall, however, my absences have strangely strengthened our marriage as her selflessness during them has heightened my respect, appreciation, and love for her.

In Christian marriage each individual's actions have an *other* focus. Manipulation, intimidation, and deceit for personal gain have no place here. Such actions will destroy true love even if they secure personal advantages for a time. The Bible simply puts before us the wonderful mystery of human happiness: in the giving of self lie life's greatest gains. The greatest love grows where self is served the least. This mystery takes concrete form in marriage when we patiently endure one another's fears and foolishness, refuse to use strengths to take advantage of another's weaknesses, enable each to fulfill responsibilities, cheer one another's dreams, comfort each other's sorrows, work to understand each other's needs, and forgive one another.

The Truths That Count

These last words about forgiveness are important, for they remind us that all these instructions *sound* easy until we disappoint, frustrate, or sin against each other—then loving actions become enormous challenges. Not only do we have trouble forgiving, but the very fact that we find this divine imperative a struggle reveals the spiritual weakness in each heart. That is why the apostle John tells us to love "in truth" as well as in deed. That "truth" involves more than dealing with one another in integrity. Each of us must also face a vital truth about ourselves: we are far less capable of selfless love than we dare to confess.

To care for another more than we do for ourselves runs counter to our nature. Personal satisfaction, control, and advancement dominate our thoughts and pursuits. Even our care for one another cannot rid itself of the motives of recompense and recognition. If you do not believe this, then simply remember the rage that filled your heart the last time you went the extra mile for a spouse or a child and no one said thank you.

Our general expectation of some return on the love we invest in another reminds us that genuine affection and willing sacrifice may still have significant measures of self in them. In fact, purely selfless love eludes us all. For who would contend that in their marriages they never do or desire anything that requires their being served by the actions or responses of a spouse? What the apostle has told us to *be* in our marriages is beyond us. Each of us fails the requirement never to manipulate, intimidate, or use another.

This truth is most evident when we consider *why* Christ died. John tells us about the sacrifice of Jesus not merely to give us an example to mimic but to remind us of our guilt that he must cover. Yet in this reminder there is more than the exposure of truth about us; there is also the revelation of a God who is *for* us. In the sacrifice of his Son, our God reveals his selfless desire to bless his children. Our God gains nothing in the deal of providing his Son to take the penalty for our guilt. His love is more selfless than that of a mother nursing her baby. She gives of herself to the child, who can do nothing for her. Our God has given his own life for us, even though we are as helpless as infants to benefit him.

Full understanding of our Lord's selflessness ultimately engenders in us those attributes lacking in our own love that will make it last. First, as we humbly contemplate the forgiveness that God freely gives us, we discover how hypocritical it is to receive undeserved pardon and then not offer it to another (see Matt. 18:21–35). Then, in recognition of our own need for forgiveness, we discover the willingness to forgive that heals and seals our relationships. This is why love has a chance despite the inescapable truth of personal selfishness that we each must confess.

A wedding sealed by forgiveness took place several years ago near New York City. A young Asian-American woman had invited her father to her wedding despite his abandonment of her mother nearly thirty years earlier when the family had arrived in the United States. As part of the wedding tradition in their country of origin, the father was to be served a meal by the young woman's mother.

Though she was a Christian, the mother protested. When her husband had left her destitute with three small children many years before, she had labored unceasingly in menial jobs to support them. At the same time she was earning multiple degrees at prestigious universities. Ultimately she earned a doctorate in child psychology and established a clinic of national repute to treat troubled children. For her, the thought of serving the man who had treated her so despicably was repulsive and humanly impossible.

For the sake of their daughter, both mother and father came to the wedding. Still, the mother made no commitment to serve the father as tradition required. She watched her husband enter the wedding room with an arrogant stride, as if he deserved to be there. She listened to him speak to relatives without shame or apology for the misery he had caused his own family. His every action and word increased the temperature of the thirty years of resentment in her.

Until the actual moment in the ceremony when the ritual meal was to occur, the mother would not agree to participate in the service. Then, though it surprised her as much as it did the others in attendance, the mother took the ceremonial bowl of rice, knelt before her husband, and served him. The rice she put on his plate was moistened by her tears. "They were not tears of pain," she later said, "but of inexpressible joy."

She explained, "When I let go of my anger enough to serve my husband, it was as though I understood for the first time how much Jesus loves me. I understood the pain he endured not to hold my eternal guilt against me but to serve me by giving his own life for me. When I served my husband, I felt the love of my Savior flood into my heart and wash away thirty years of fury that had embittered me and enslaved my heart. In forgiveness I found freedom from the misery in my heart that I had not been able to erase with all of my achievements."

More was achieved by the forgiveness she displayed than the mother initially knew. When the daughter witnessed the selflessness of her mother, she later said that for the first time she believed the love of God was so real that it could have power in her own marriage. The daughter's unvoiced fear that her faults or her husband's would ultimately destroy their happiness, as it had her parents', evaporated in the knowledge that Christ's forgiveness could be shared. The forgiveness the mother demonstrated freed her own heart to love again and sealed the love of her daughter's marriage.

As wonderful as it is to discover and share the truths of our Savior's forgiveness, this is not the end of our blessing. As we forgive others and our perception of the reality of our Savior's pardon deepens, our desire to honor him naturally increases. Then as we honor him with our lives, something else very special happens. We discover to our delight that by loving the Lord who created marriage, our love for our spouses has the greatest opportunity to grow.

When our first son was small, he loved to walk through the church parking lot between his mother and me. We would each hold one of his hands, and then on cue he would lift his feet. He would giggle while his legs dangled in the air between us. But he would whoop for pure joy when we would swing him back and forth until his feet actually went above our heads. The higher we swung him, the greater was his delight.

Something else also happened with each swing of our child. Not only did Kathy and I lift our son higher, but we were inevitably drawn closer together by the physical forces engaged in doing so. When two lives in a marriage lift the Son of God in honor, similar dynamics occur—the higher we lift him, the closer together we grow. By honoring him, our hearts are changed, our priorities come more in line with his purposes, our selfishness withers, and our forgiveness grows. We begin to tolerate each other's weaknesses more because we recognize our need for Christ's sufficiency in our own weaknesses. Our mutual understanding of each other deepens because we are each becoming more like Christ—for his glory and for our spouse's sake.

A Third Party

The commitments that we make in marriage are not merely agreements between two people. Christ, in actively renewing and deepening the love that we share, is also a party to our relationship. This truth further secures Christian marriages.

When we vow to love and honor each other, we also make these promises *before* and *to* our God. This means that even when words and feelings between the two people fail to keep the marriage that God desires, we should not consider the marriage finished. Our promises to remain perpetually committed to each other are ultimately made to God.

If we have given our lives to the purpose of reflecting God's character and commitments, then in our marriage vows we promise God that we will live for the other person. God does not make his love conditional on the way we feel about him, on how we treat him, or on whether we have failed him. Thus neither the cooling of our affections for another nor the heat of stress with that person excuses us from our marriage commitments. We live for another because we have committed ourselves to living for the God who requires it. We love another because we promised the God we love that we would.

Because the actions that keep a Christian couple united are linked to their eternal commitments to God, their marriage becomes a haven for the constant renewal of love rather than a trap to escape when an initial ardor dies. The man and woman need not be constantly questioning if either will say or do something that destroys their relationship; rather, they proceed to live with freedom and boldness in the knowledge that their mutual commitment to God has secured their home more surely than their affections ever could. Yet, curiously, it is this very security that gives their affections the greatest potential to deepen. Committing to love another person beyond his or her weaknesses, to work on a relationship despite difficulties and differences, and to live for the other because that's what God requires, gives love the richest soil possible in which to flourish.

Consider that no matter how happy your marriage is now, this may only be the beginning of the joy that you can know as you entrust your lives to the Lord. He will use your shared love for him to increase your love for each other. And in marriages where love for God is not shared, God can still use your love for your spouse to deepen your appreciation of God's unconditional care for you, to teach your spouse the nature of God's care through you, and even to stimulate in your spouse renewed love for God and you (see 1 Peter 3:1–2). By living—and sacrificing—for another's welfare, each person reflects the love of the Savior and becomes Christ's representative in the home.

Such sacrificial love is not secured by words that we mouth nor even by actions that we initiate under some romantic impulse to make another (or ourselves) feel good. The love that is truly secure stems from hearts united with God through Christ. Because words can ring hollow and actions can spring from motives hidden even to the one who acts, only our hearts' commitments to Christ will turn our words and actions into the marriage we most desire. Our spiritual commitments—what is deepest in our hearts rather than the outward expressions of words or deeds—ultimately will secure what is dearest in our lives.

We should not be surprised that what is inside is most important. Our experience regularly tells us to beware of external appearances when assessing true integrity. Our nation has just marked the twentieth anniversary of the tragedy of the *Challenger* space shuttle. Investigators went to amazing lengths to discern the cause of the spaceship's explosion that led to the deaths of seven astronauts. Ultimately experts found that in the unusually cold temperatures of that day, gaskets—known as O-rings—around the engines had failed. The failure caused a fuel leak that ignited and led to the shuttle's explosion.

Initially this analysis surprised some at NASA because inspectors had externally examined the O-rings just prior to the flight. Everything looked fine on the outside. What the disaster investigation revealed was that the external inspection was not meaningful. The tragedy was due to failures on the inside of those rings where no one could see.

On our wedding days, most of us put on another kind of ring. The words that we say and the actions that we take to put the golden bands in place make everything appear fine on the outside. We must remember that what is inside counts more. The commitment of our hearts to the grace of God ultimately makes our words and actions truly and eternally loving. Living for the one who loved us when we were yet his enemies teaches us what it means for each to live for the other in marriage when no other earthly cause may justify our continuing union. The Lord who died for us teaches us that when we give of ourselves for another—dying to ourselves in the process—we discover what it really means to live and enjoy most fully what it really means to love. Our Lord makes our lives as sweet as heaven desires by drawing our hearts together in love for him.

Conclusion

ONLY WEEKS AFTER Kathy and I were married, we had one of the most difficult arguments of our lives. I cannot now even remember what the subject was. All I can remember were the hours of discussion, the mounds of tear-drying tissues heaped on the bed, the lateness of the evening, and Kathy's final question: "If we have this kind of difference between us, is our marriage over?"

I then did one of the dumbest things I have ever done in my life. I laughed—not just a chuckle but a deep, long, bellyaching, sidesplitting roar. I am sure that my reaction was, in part, an involuntary release of the tension built up in me, but it was also a response to how hilarious I considered Kathy's question. The thought had never entered my mind that our differences were a threat to our marriage. I loved Kathy more than I could well express. I was looking forward to spending a lifetime with her. I had promised God that I would love her regardless of difficulty. The suggestion that an argument might undo us struck me as so off-the-wall and bizarre that I could not help but laugh.

I am not suggesting that laughing was the right thing to do, but God graciously used it that night to reassure Kathy of the security of our relationship. Seeing that the idea of some disagreement separating us was so foreign to me that I could not keep from laughing at it gave her a sense of how secure she was in our relationship. Her knowledge of that security made her more willing to bring up other things in the future that we needed to discuss. These were not always pleasant discussions, but they enabled us to deal with matters that ultimately have made our marriage far stronger and sweeter.

God used Kathy's and my commitment to him to make our marriage so secure that we could work on our weaknesses, growing past them to increase the quality of our love for each other. We still have much growing that we need to do. But we do not fear growing because God has taught us that by committing our lives to honoring him, we invite his care into our marriage to help deepen our love for him and each other. His care brings us closer with each passing year, not only through the unusual (like my laughter) but by placing us in situations that enable us to understand each other better. He lets us see how our lives can touch others, and so we learn to appreciate each other's gifts. He unites our hearts to pray for our children's battles and blessings, and he gives us enough trials to keep us tender with enough joys to keep us hugging. In all of this the bond of love between us is strengthened because through all of it we learn more of how to represent Christ to one another as he has given himself for us.

We cannot say that we know how it has happened at every step, but Kathy and I marvel that in each phase of our marriage we grow closer and consider our relationship a greater blessing. We know too much about our own weaknesses to credit ourselves for this grace. We simply praise God that when we are weak, he is strong. He continues to teach us of our Savior's love—despite our brokenness—to teach us how we should love one another. As we have grown in appreciation of the grace each of us needs, our Lord has increasingly enabled us to overlook weaknesses, forgive faults, and appreciate mutual foibles. For this reason we humbly rejoice that we will never have to look back on our wedding day or our first years together as the best time of our marriage. As we understand and express more of Christ's grace, we are able more and more to rejoice in each other, and our love gets better and better. Through Christ the best days of our love are always ahead. Our prayer and the purpose of this book is to help others partake of similar blessings.

DISCUSSION QUESTIONS

Introduction: Who's in Charge?

1. What motivations other than sacrifice can govern the relationships of men and women?
2. How does the grace of God become a reality in our homes through sacrifice?
3. Why does knowledge of Bible facts alone not adequately prepare us for the home life God intends?
4. What will adequately prepare us for the home life God intends?
5. What are challenges in our society to the Bible's instruction for the family?
6. Why is self-sacrifice the cornerstone of the Bible's architecture for the Christian home?
7. Does living for another require an abandonment of one's integrity or authority?

Chapter 1: A Man's Responsibility

1. How does Paul compare the relationship of a husband and wife to that of Christ and the church?

2. How does the biblical concept of "headship" contradict philosophies of self-serving male passivity or dominance?
3. In what sense does biblical headship involve authority?
4. In what sense does biblical headship involve service?
5. What is a servant/leader? Who best models this role in Scripture? How?
6. In what ways does the head of a home dispense grace into the home?

Chapter 2: God's Reasons for Servant Leadership

1. How is the servant/leader role of a husband related to the redemptive purposes of marriage?
2. In what sense is improper biblical headship spiritual robbery?
3. Why is the devaluing of one's spouse always spiritually self-destructive? To whom else is it spiritually destructive? Why?
4. In what sense does a wife complete her husband? How does this affect a man's expression of biblical headship?
5. What are some ways that a husband can honor his wife? Why is it important to do so? How does a husband's honoring of his wife affect him?
6. In what ways does biblical headship honor God?

Chapter 3: God's Resources for Servant Leadership

1. How is selflessness a resource for husbands to express headship in the home?

2. How can husbands foster growth in their wives? Why should husbands do this?

3. How does a husband's character affect the spiritual health of his wife?

4. Does the Bible mandate a specific manner or personality for the proper expression of headship?

5. In what way does one's relationship with Christ affect one's ability to act as the biblical head of a home? How is humility related to headship?

6. What kinds of insecurities may cause a man to want his wife dependent on him?

7. When and why is it good for a husband to lose an argument (or discussion)?

8. How does the leadership and sacrifice of Christ instruct husbands in their headship role?

Chapter 4: A Woman's Responsibility

1. What analogy and example does Paul use to express how wives should submit to their husbands?

2. To what extent does the apostle say wives should submit to husbands?

3. Is the instruction given in this passage to husbands and wives culturally limited? What is the basis for your conclusion?

4. In what sense does biblical submission require one to complete another?

5. In what sense does biblical submission require one to glorify another?

6. Does submission require the suppression of one's gifts, talents, and abilities? If not, why not?

7. Are there any limits to how one's gifts, talents, and abilities should be expressed? If so, what are these limits and how are they determined?

Chapter 5: A Woman's Dignity

1. How does biblical submission grant a wife dignity?
2. Does biblical submission lessen the value or worth of anyone in God's estimation? If not, why not?
3. In what ways does a focus on promoting ourselves rob us of dignity?
4. Why are almost any career or family choices a woman makes in today's world attackable?
5. How should the church affirm the dignity and gifts of Christian women?
6. How should a Christian husband demonstrate respect for a wife who lives in accord with Scripture?

Chapter 6: A Woman's Desire

1. In what ways are wives tempted to neglect or break Scripture's command to respect their husbands?
2. In what ways should Christian wives respect their husbands? Why?
3. How can a woman respect a husband who is not worthy of such regard?
4. How can a woman respect a man who does not respect her? Should she respect such a man? In what ways?

5. What does the Bible mean when it tells Christian wives to "reverence" their husbands? Why do you think the apostle uses this language?

6. Why is it important not to base regard for a spouse on his or her worthiness?

7. What influence does a godly wife exert on her family, church, and community? How important is this influence?

Chapter 7: Parental Foundations

1. In what ways does parents' involvement in the life of the church aid their parenting?

2. In what ways does our perception of God as our Father shape the parents we are able to be?

3. In what ways does our security (or insecurity) in Christ affect our parenting?

4. How does the relationship of a husband and wife bring the reality of Christ's love into a home?

5. How important is the relationship of a husband and wife on the physical and emotional health of children?

6. How important is the relationship of a husband and wife on the spiritual health of children? Why?

Chapter 8: Parental Responsibilities

1. To whom does Scripture give the responsibility for child rearing? How should this responsibility affect parents' priorities regarding their work, energy, time, and attention?

2. Which parent is ultimately accountable for a child's nurture in a two-parent household? Does this mean that one parent is not accountable for a child's nurture? Explain.
3. What does the apostle mean when he instructs parents, "Do not exasperate your children"? What are ways parents exasperate their children?
4. How important is parental discipline for the physical, social, and spiritual health of children?
5. What keeps parents from disciplining their children?
6. How does our security in Christ affect our ability to parent fairly and consistently?
7. How is firm but kindly discipline prescribed in Scripture? How is it manifested in parenting? How is it mangled in parenting?

Chapter 9: Each for the Other Forever

1. Why can words not secure a marriage, even if we mean them?
2. What kinds of actions secure love?
3. How does Christ's forgiveness of us affect our actions toward our spouses?
4. Who is the third party in every marriage vow, and how does this person affect our marriage commitments?
5. Why does a person's commitment to Christ affect his or her words and actions in marriage?
6. Why should one spouse live out his or her commitments to Christ if the other spouse does not?
7. How can married love keep getting better and better?

Notes

Introduction

1. National Vital Statistic Reports, vol. 54, no. 2 (September 28, 2005): 2; see R. M. Kreider, "Number, Timing, and Duration of Marriages and Divorces: 2001," tables 3, 9; Current Population Reports, P70–97 (2005), Washington DC: U.S. Census Bureau; National Center for Health Statistics, vol. 52, no. 20 (2004): 1120; Arlene Saluter and Terry Lugaila, "Marital Status and Living Arrangements: March 1996," U.S. Department of Commerce, U.S. Census Bureau, Population Division, PPL-67.

Chapter 1: A Man's Responsibility

1. The man is also described as the head of the woman in 1 Corinthians 11:3–10. Other key passages on this subject include Genesis 2:18–25; 3:16; 1 Corinthians 14:33–35; Colossians 3:18; 1 Timothy 2:8–15; Titus 2:3–5; 1 Peter 3:1–6.

2. James B. Hurley, *Man and Woman in Biblical Perspective* (Grand Rapids: Zondervan, 1981), 167–81, 254–71.

3. These issues are well explored and explained in Hurley, *Man and Woman in Biblical Perspective*, 181–84; S. M. Baugh, "A Foreign World: Ephesus in the First Century," in *Women in the Church: A*

Fresh Analysis of 1 Timothy 2:9–15, ed. Andreas J. Kostenberger, Thomas H. Schreiner, and H. Scott Baldwin (Grand Rapids: Baker, 1995), 47–48; Thomas H. Schreiner, "An Interpretation of 1 Timothy 2:9–15: A Dialogue with Scholarship," in *Women in the Church*, 117–21; John Piper and Wayne Grudem, "An Overview of Central Concerns," in *Recovering Biblical Manhood and Womanhood*, ed. John Piper and Wayne Grudem (Wheaton: Crossway, 1991), 65–67, 74–75; Edmund P. Clowney, "The Church," in *Contours of Christian Theology*, gen. ed. Gerald Bray (Downers Grove, IL: InterVarsity Press, 1995), 215–35.

4. William J. Larkin Jr., *Culture and Biblical Hermeneutics* (Grand Rapids: Baker, 1988), 109.

5. A noteworthy early article thrusting this idea into popular evangelical discussion is Berkeley and Alvera Mickelsen, "The 'Head' of the Epistles," *Christianity Today* 25, no. 4 (February 20, 1981): 21ff. Similar discussions appear in the Mickelsens' later work, "What Does *Kephale* Mean in the New Testament?" in *Women, Authority and the Bible*, ed. Alvera Mickelsen (Downers Grove, IL: InterVarsity Press, 1986), 97–110. Other related articles also appear in this source, pages 111–32, 134–54. See also Catherine Clark Kroeger, "The Classical Concept of *Head* as 'Source,'" appendix 3 in Gretchen Gaebelein Hull, *Equal to Serve* (Old Tappan, NJ: Revell, 1987), 267–83.

6. Michael Ovey, "Equality but Not Symmetry: Women, Men and the Nature of God," *The Cambridge Papers* 1, no. 2 (June 1992): 2–3.

7. Wayne Grudem, "Does *Kephale* ('Head') Mean 'Source' or 'Authority Over' in Greek Literature? A Survey of 2,336 Examples," in *The Role Relationship of Men and Women*, ed. George Knight III (Chicago: Moody, 1985), 50. See also Grudem's later discussion in Piper and Grudem, *Recovering Biblical Manhood and Womanhood*, 63–64, 425–68; and Susan T. Foh, *Women and the Word of God: A Response to Biblical Feminism* (Phillipsburg, NJ: Presbyterian and Reformed, 1979), 101–2.

8. F. F. Bruce, *The Epistle to the Colossians, to Philemon, and to the Ephesians* (Grand Rapids: Eerdmans, 1984), 384. Further

reasons for the "authority" translation are discussed by Thomas H. Schreiner, Harold O. J. Brown, and Daniel Doriani in *Women in the Church*, 135–46, 200–206, 259–67.

9. Though more able language scholars than I have studied this question, it appears to me that the term *head* may in certain verses *include* the idea of "source" (see Hurley, *Man and Woman in Biblical Perspective*, 144–47, 164–68). However, when this is the case, "source" is not the exclusive meaning of the term but rather is a corollary, meaning contributing rationale to why the head has authority (see 1 Cor. 11:8–10; Eph. 4:14–16; Col. 1:18; 2:19). Grudem has a similar conclusion in Piper and Grudem, *Recovering Biblical Manhood and Womanhood*, 468. See also S. Bedale, "The Meaning of Kephale in the Pauline Epistles," *Journal of Theological Studies* 5 (1954): 211–15 as cited in Hurley, *Man and Woman in Biblical Perspective*, 164; and the note on Ephesians 5:23 in the *New Geneva Study Bible*, gen. ed. R. C. Sproul (Nashville: Thomas Nelson, 1995), 1869.

10. Hurley, *Man and Woman in Biblical Perspective*, 168.

11. R. Kent Hughes, *Ephesians: The Mystery of the Body of Christ* (Wheaton: Crossway, 1990), 181–82.

12. Hurley, *Man and Woman in Biblical Perspective*, 240–42.

13. The string of participles composing this long Greek sentence, though translated as imperatives, are actually descriptions of the necessary characteristics of those "filled with the Spirit."

14. Significantly different interpretations have been given to the loving phrase "submit to one another." Some have taken the phrase to mean that among Christians no one should have any authority over anyone. This interpretation seems unlikely since wives are immediately told to submit to their husbands, children are told to obey parents, and slaves (better interpreted as "servants"; see note 3 in chapter 5) are told to obey earthly masters. In addition, Paul here and elsewhere establishes offices of authority in the church (see Eph. 4:11; 1 Tim. 5:17).

Other respected interpreters examine the use of these words elsewhere and conclude the phrase applies only to those who are in submissive roles (see Hurley, *Man and Woman in Biblical Per-*

spective, 140–44; Piper and Grudem, *Recovering Biblical Manhood and Womanhood*, 493–94 [footnote 6]). This may seem to indicate that the only ones who have submission obligations are those in subservient positions. While I understand the concern these conscientious authors have not to blur biblical husband/wife distinctions by allowing that husbands are to "submit" to their wives, questions remain about their interpretation. Reasons for such questions: (1) the long Greek sentence (Eph. 5:18–21) that includes this requirement of submission also includes three other requirements that apply to *all* in the church rather than one group of persons; (2) each of these requirements is a consequence of individuals being "filled with the Spirit"—a quality *all* believers are to desire; and (3) the commands for *all* persons that follow (including husbands, parents, and masters) make it clear that putting self-interest beneath the interests of others is required of every believer (see George W. Knight III, "Husbands and Wives as Analogues of Christ and the Church: Ephesians 5:21–33 and Colossians 3:18–19," in Piper and Grudem, eds., *Recovering Biblical Manhood and Womanhood*, 167–68). Arguing that the Greek word for submission "is never 'mutual' in its force; it is *always one-directional* in its reference to submission to authority" (Piper and Grudem, 493) does not negate the possibility that submission requirements apply to all believers since each is acting "out of reverence for Christ" and thus all are ultimately submitting to the one divine authority.

My understanding is that Paul intended for the general phrase "submitting to one another out of reverence for Christ" to apply to all in the church as each lives sacrificially in every position or relationship God provides. However, with precisely inspired balance and to avoid confusion about roles and responsibilities, the apostle never uses the "submit" term when directly instructing husbands, parents, and masters about their relationships with those under their authority. The issues are complex, however, and I freely concede an unwillingness to claim certainty on the particular point of whether the specific "submit" term applies to those in authority. Still, this discussion about whether the specific term applies to all persons in every relationship should not make anyone uncertain about Paul's clear statement at the outset of this passage that all believers should "live a life of love, just as Christ loved us and gave himself up for us" (Eph. 5:2). This foundation principle makes it clear that *all* persons are to sacrifice their own interests to the purposes of God as they are being fulfilled in others.

The general requirement of personal selflessness is reemphasized when the apostle later tells those in authority to give of themselves for the good of those under their care. Hence, husbands are told to love their wives "just as Christ loved the church and gave himself up for her" (5:25; and note also that this is precisely how women are told to "submit" in 1 Peter 3:1; see 3:7); fathers are told, "do not exasperate your children" (Eph. 6:4); and masters are commanded "in the same way" not to threaten their servants since "he who is both their Master and yours is in heaven, and there is no favoritism with him" (v. 9). Paul does not obliterate all authority but rather requires all persons of every distinction to surrender their own advantages and benefits to the good of the ones for whom they are responsible. The closest analogy to this kind of submission is the very one that Paul is citing (i.e., in love Christ served the church by sacrificing himself in her behalf, but in terms of authority he did not serve the church in the same way that she submits to him). He maintained his authority even as he humbled himself to offer his life for the church's good (see Phil. 2:5–11). For expert discussion of this careful balance, see Foh, *Women and the Word of God*, 134.

15. Note also that since the pivotal verses in the Ephesians passage (which require loving sacrifice of all persons in all positions) hold the controlling thought for the concepts that follow, it is appropriate that "servant" have the priority position in the servant/leader terminology (see Eph. 5:1–2, 18–21).

16. Hughes, *Ephesians*, 184.

Chapter 2: God's Reasons for Servant Leadership

1. Geoffrey C. Ward with Ric Burns and Ken Burns, *The Civil War: An Illustrated History* (New York: Alfred A. Knopf, 1990), 82–83.

2. Writes Charles E. Mylander, "Beware of emotional delight outside of marriage that is not taking place within it. An emotional affair precedes a physical one. The first step toward adultery is discovering a special pleasure with someone of the opposite sex other than one's spouse. During this 'conversation stage' everything seems innocent and fun—until the friendship begins to seem more fulfilling than your marriage." See Charles E. Mylander, "Running the Yellow Lights," *Marriage Partnership* 4, no. 6 (November–December 1987): 36–38.

3. Though sometimes ridiculed as "the gift nobody wants," the Bible identifies celibacy (i.e., living singly because of the circumstances or calling God has arranged for one's life) as an honored relationship with God. Those God calls to singleness as evidenced by their desires or their circumstances are the only ones who are designed (i.e., gifted) by God to be complete without being in union with a spouse. Such persons are, in a special sense, married to God. They find their wholeness in him without the need of another's help or support in the marital union (see Gen. 2:18; 1 Cor. 11:11). As a result, those gifted for singleness are specially equipped to serve God without the encumbering responsibilities the married must consider (see Matt. 19:10–12; 1 Cor. 7:4–7, 25–38). The Bible does not indicate that any calling is without its challenges, but the fact that celibacy is a gift of God grants the status honor and dignity despite the attitudes of a society or the struggles of those who are single.

Elisabeth Elliot writes, "The gift of virginity, given to everyone to offer back to God for His use, is a priceless and irreplaceable gift. It can be offered in the pure sacrifice of marriage, or it can be offered in the sacrifice of a life's celibacy. Does this sound just too high and holy? But think a moment—because the virgin has never known a man, she is free to concern herself wholly with God's affairs, as Paul said in 1 Corinthians 7, 'and her aim in life is to make herself holy, in body and spirit.' She keeps her heart as the Bride of Christ in a very special sense, and offers to the Heavenly Bridegroom alone all that she is and has. When she gives herself willingly to Him in love she has no need to justify herself to the world or to Christians who plague her with questions and suggestions. In a way not open to the married woman her daily 'living sacrifice' is a powerful and humble witness, radiating love. I believe she may enter into the 'mystery' more deeply than the rest of us." See "Virginity," *Elisabeth Elliot Newsletter* (Ann Arbor, MI: Servant Publications [March–April 1990]): 2–3.

4. Tertullian, as quoted in David and Vera Mace, *What's Happening to Clergy Marriages?* (Nashville: Abingdon, 1980), 97.

Chapter 3: God's Resources for Servant Leadership

1. Karen Howe, "Husbands, Forget the Heroics!" *Eternity* 25, no. 12 (December 1974): 11.

2. Robertson McQuilkin, "Living by Vows," *Christianity Today* 39, no. 14 (October 8, 1990): 38–40.

3. Paul Tournier, *To Understand Each Other* (Richmond: John Knox, 1967), 22–26, 38–42.

4. Howe, 12.

5. The first response in the historic *Westminster Shorter Catechism* is "Man's chief end is to glorify God and enjoy him forever." See Matthew 22:37.

6. "He has showed you, O man, what is good. And what does the LORD require of you? To act justly and to love mercy and to walk humbly with your God" (Micah 6:8). See earlier definitions of biblical headship, pp. 35–41.

7. Robertson McQuilkin, "Muriel's Blessing," *Christianity Today* 40, no. 2 (February 5, 1996): 34. Muriel died in September 2003.

8. McQuilkin, "Living by Vows," 40.

Chapter 4: A Woman's Responsibility

1. Hal Farnsworth, now a pastor in Athens, Georgia.

2. See Genesis 2:18–25; 3:16; 1 Corinthians 11:3–16; 14:33–36; Ephesians 5:22–33; Colossians 3:18; 1 Timothy 2:8–15; Titus 2:3–5; 1 Peter 3:1–6.

3. See 1 Peter 2:17; 3:7. The New Testament word for *respect* in these passages has a range of meaning determined by context as does our modern equivalent (for example, children who respect

their father and respect the president are not expected to hum "Hail to the Chief" each time Dad enters a room). Nevertheless, the Bible makes it clear that husbands must treat their wives with the consideration due those for whom Christ gave his blood.

4. The Greek word for submission is a combination of *tasso*, meaning "to arrange," "to put in order," or "to command," and *hupo*, meaning "under." Still, we must take care to interpret all words in the Bible not merely in accord with their background meanings but in the light of their context and biblical use. Standard Greek references will interpret *hupotasso* in the forms that occur in these passages as meaning "to be subject, subordinate, or submissive." See Hurley, *Man and Woman in Biblical Perspective*, 142–46.

5. Piper and Grudem, "An Overview of Central Concerns," 61; Knight, "Husbands and Wives," 166; Schreiner, "An Interpretation of 1 Timothy 2:9–15," 125. Note this last definition is based on the parallel phrasing in 1 Timothy 2:11–12.

6. Marion Stroud, *I Love God and My Husband* (Wheaton: Victor, 1973), 53.

7. Virtually all commentators quickly add that submission is not an unqualified mandate to obey a spouse if such submission would require transgression of God's standards. See Foh, *Women and the Word of God*, 184. Susan Hunt writes, "Women are not to submit to sin. Sometimes it is very clear when that line has been crossed. Sometimes the line, or the vision of the line, is blurred. When the authority of the husband cannot be trusted, I encourage women to seek the advice, authority, and protection of the elders of her church" (Susan Hunt, *The True Woman* [Wheaton: Crossway, 1997], 206).

8. See earlier discussion in chapter 2 on the "gift of celibacy" and Foh, *Women and the Word of God*, 128–29.

9. See, for example, Psalms 10:14; 28:7 (in Hebrew); 54:3–4; 72:12; 86:17. Susan Hunt in *The True Woman* comments on the impact of such references for wives: "This explanation of how God is our ezer [Helper] gives us insight into the helper role. The ways that God is our Helper can be summarized into two categories: community and compassion. God enters into a loving, protect-

ing relationship with his people (community). He comes to our aid, comforts us and is merciful toward us (compassion). . . . This touches our feminine souls because our entering into nurturing relationships, and extending compassion to those in need, is part of our helper design. Our design equips us to infuse community and compassion into our relationships. Women will do this in various ways. We are not clones. Our strengths, temperaments, experiences, opportunities, life-stage, and interests will be factors in how we fulfill this design" (p. 206). For an explanation of how the "helper" term does not imply inferiority, see Foh, *Women and the Word of God*, 60.

10. Elisabeth Elliot, "The Essence of Femininity: A Personal Perspective," in *Recovering Biblical Manhood and Womanhood*, 397.

11. This understanding fits with Piper and Grudem's conclusion that "submission refers to a wife's divine calling to honor and affirm her husband's leadership and help carry it through according to her gifts," in *Recovering Biblical Manhood and Womanhood*, 61.

12. John Stott, *God's New Society* (Downers Grove, IL: InterVarsity Press, 1979), 219.

13. Hughes, *Ephesians*, 185.

14. Susan Foh in *Women and the Word of God* writes, "The Christian wife has the responsibility to grow in Christ, to know doctrine, to be able to speak the truth in love. . . . In addition, she is not to be silent when her husband sins (Matt. 18:15), but she is to teach and admonish him (Col. 3:16). However, she is to do all of these things with a submissive heart. . . . The Christian wife is neither passive nor mindless. She does not have to pretend that her husband is always right or hide her own talents or intelligence. She is to use her gifts for the upbuilding of the body of Christ, which includes her husband" (p. 186).

Chapter 5: A Woman's Dignity

1. Paul Settle, "One in Christ," *Equip for Ministry* 2, no. 4 (July–August 1996): 16.

2. See the manuscript data in *The Greek New Testament* of the United Bible Societies; and George W. Knight III, "Husbands and

Wives as Analogues of Christ and the Church: Ephesians 5:21–33 and Colossians 3:18–19," in *Recovering Biblical Manhood and Womanhood*, 166.

3. Though Paul addresses "slaves" here (as Peter does in the parallel 1 Peter 2:18), we are wrong if we interpret the words only in the context of the despicable, chattel slavery of American history. The word translated "slave" in this passage most naturally refers to household servants, which included those in apprentice and indentured relationships as well as captured enemies and employed servants. Thus Peter's instruction applies to all who by reason of training, occupation, or situation had their lives controlled by another. The spectrum of persons being addressed makes it appropriate for us to apply these words to modern employment situations.

4. The observation that the Bible never specifically tells husbands to submit to wives is an important caution for those who wish to say that the command to "submit to one another" removes all gender distinctions in the church. Far from removing respective authority/submission responsibilities in the home, the apostles are of one voice in the precise way they maintain the Bible's commitment to husband-headship and wife-submission while carefully contextualizing the expression of these roles in Christ's sacrificial use of authority and his noble example of submission. See note in Piper and Grudem, eds., *Recovering Biblical Manhood and Womanhood*, 493.

5. Note that in 1 Peter 3:7 the apostle commands husbands to treat their wives with *respect*, the same word he uses a few verses earlier (2:17) to describe how we should treat kings, among others.

6. David B. Calhoun, *Faith and Learning 1812–1868*, vol. 1 of *History of Princeton Seminary* (Edinburgh, UK: Banner of Truth Trust, 1994), 173.

7. See the *Westminster Shorter Catechism*, question 6.

8. Ovey, "Equality but Not Symmetry," 1–4.

9. Susan Hunt in *The True Woman* offers this helpful commentary: "[E]very woman is not to submit to every man, but every married woman is to submit to her husband. The Scriptural command to women is . . . to 'be submissive to your husbands' (1 Peter 3:1). In

Titus 2 we read that older women are to teach younger women to 'be subject to their husbands' . . . [T]he Biblical commands about women not usurping authority have reference to the home and church, not society in general" (p. 206).

10. Phoebe Hoban, "Women Who Run with the Trends," *Harper's Bazaar* (January 1994): 42.

11. A point articulately made by UCLA professor Patricia Marks Greenfield in "The Missing Half of Feminism," *St. Louis Post-Dispatch*, December 26, 1996, p. 7B.

12. Gary and Betsy Ricucci, as quoted in Gary Thomas, *Sacred Marriage* (Grand Rapids: Zondervan, 2000), 182.

13. John Angell James, *Female Piety* (1860; reprint, Pittsburgh: Soli Deo Gloria, 1994), 72.

Chapter 6: A Woman's Desire

1. Hunt, *The True Woman*, 103.

2. God speaks to Eve of her changed nature after sinning, saying, "Your desire will be for your husband" (Gen. 3:16). The words do not refer to her physical desire alone, for prior to her sin God had blessed both man and wife with sexual attraction. Rather, the words refer to a woman's now corrupted desire for the man's very essence—control of his position, being, and heart, which (as the Genesis account of the fall has already made clear) is self-destructive to individuals and relationships. That the issue is actually control and not attraction is made clear by the words that follow: "Your desire will be for your husband, [but] he will rule over you." Compare the similar wording in Genesis 4:7. For a fuller discussion of these issues, see Ray C. Ortlund Jr., "Male-Female Equality and Male Headship in Genesis 1–3," in *Recovering Biblical Manhood and Womanhood*, 108–9; Clowney, *The Church*, 219.

3. Gary Thomas, *Sacred Marriage* (Grand Rapids: Zondervan, 2000), 188–89.

4. Statistics from "The Effectiveness of Couples Treatment for Spouse Abuse," *Journal of Marital and Family Therapy* 29, no. 3 (July 2003): 407–26.

Part 3: Sacrificial Partners

1. Hunt, *The True Woman*, 30–32.

Chapter 7: Parental Foundations

1. William Willimon, "Reaching and Teaching the Abandoned Generation," *Christian Century* 11, no. 29 (October 20, 1993): 1018.

Chapter 8: Parental Responsibilities

1. Willimon, "Reaching and Teaching," 1018.
2. David Blankenhorn, *Fatherless America* (New York: Basic Books, 1995), 2, 18–19. Blankenhorn cites that in 1960, 80.6 percent of children in America were living with both parents; in 1990, the percentage was 57.7. In 1960, the percentage of children living only with their mother was 7.7 percent; in 1990, the percentage rose to 21.6. In 1990, 36.3 percent of America's children were living apart from their biological fathers. By the year 2000, half of our children were growing up without fathers present daily.
3. Bonnidell Clouse, *Teaching for Moral Growth* (Wheaton: Victor, 1993), 67–68.

Bryan and Kathy Chapell have been married for almost thirty years. He is an author of award-winning books, a pastor, and current president of Covenant Theological Seminary. She is a choir director, gifted flute player, and caring listener for many. They are the parents of Colin, Jordan, Corinne, and Kaitlin.

To receive a copy of a small-group leader's guide for *Each for the Other*, contact the Media Office at Covenant Theological Seminary, 12330 Conway Road, St. Louis, MO 63141, 314-434-4044 (www.covenantseminary.edu). You may also download a free copy from www.bryanchapell.com, where other resources from Dr. Chapell are also available.

Also by Bryan Chapell

Christ-Centered Preaching
Holiness by Grace
I'll Love You Anyway and Always
Praying Backwards
Standing Your Ground
The Promises of Grace
The Wonder of It All
Using Illustrations to Preach with Power

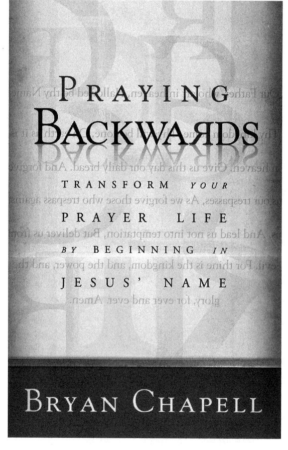